A CRITICAL ANALYSIS OF THE CONTRIBUTIONS OF NOTABLE BLACK ECONOMISTS

Dedicated to my father, E.K. Quartey,
a true African scholar.

A Critical Analysis of the Contributions of Notable Black Economists

KOJO A. QUARTEY
College of Business and Professional Studies
Lincoln University, Missouri

ASHGATE

Published by
Ashgate Publishing Limited
Gower House
Croft Road
Aldershot
Hampshire GU11 3HR
England

Ashgate Publishing Company
Suite 420
101 Cherry Street
Burlington, VT 05401-4405
USA

Ashgate website:http://www.ashgate.com

British Library Cataloguing in Publication Data
Quartey, Kojo A.
   A critical analysis of the contributions of notable black
   economists. - (Interdisciplinary research series in ethnic,
   gender and class relations)
   1. Afro-American economists 2. Economists - Africa
   3. Economics - United States - History
   I. Title
   330'.092396

Library of Congress Control Number: 00-134483

ISBN 1 84014 147 6

Printed and bound by Athenaeum Press, Ltd.,
Gateshead, Tyne & Wear.

Contents

Preface

When Sir W. Arthur Lewis won the Nobel Prize in economics in 1979, I was a freshman in college. I went on to study economics and obtain a doctoral degree in the field. During that time I studied the history of economic thought and heard only limited reference to the 'British economist.' It was not until 1989, ten years after Lewis' crowning achievement, that I realized he was black. As ironic as it may seem, while teaching a course in the history of economic thought at historically black Talladega College, I saw a footnote reference to Lewis in the textbook I was using. He was referred to as the individual who 'shared the Nobel Prize with Schultz in 1979.' The section was on Theodore Schultz, and this was the only reference made to Lewis in the entire text. Fortunately, this has been rectified in subsequent editions and liberal coverage has been given to his theories.

That experience was the catalyst for the conception of the idea for and the inception of this book. After delivering several papers on the subject and one or two minor publications, I embarked on this project. It is an attempt to give proper credit to the great black scholars of antiquity and our times, and allow them to take their rightful place in the history of economic thought. Yes, economics can be a noble profession, even for young black children.

It seems paradoxical that worldwide we idolize sports figures and entertainers, yet give little honor to theorists and scholars who shape our minds. While parents want their children to grow up to be sports stars, doctors, lawyers, and even politicians, do parents want their children to become economists? Perhaps, many do not understand what economists do or that economics can lead to great prosperity and fame. As we study the evolution of economic thought through the ages, it is quite easy to overlook the contributions of those who are in the minority. Is it that minorities have made little or no contributions to economics? Or have not enough minorities made significant contributions?

There are some great role model economists, both historical and contemporary, who are worthy of emulation by young blacks, especially those who are aspiring economists. This study looks at the works of such individuals. They include a Nobel Laureate, a former president (Ghana), an international scholar, a university president and a female pioneer, among others.

We hear of black scientists, artists, entertainers, etc. What about black economists? The major purpose of this study is to highlight the achievements of these prominent black economists and to critically analyze their contributions to economic theory, as well as other significant contributions. The individuals included in this study were all trained as economists and have made contributions to the theory and to the black community. The analyses of their contributions are intended to shed more light on those theories and thoughts, and are meant to be more analytical than critical.

We begin by briefly looking at the contributions of Africans to philosophy and economic thought. For centuries, Africans have made numerous contributions to scholarly thought. This, in many instances, has largely gone unrecognized. Theophile Obenga (Sertima, 1993) speaks of Pharaohic Egyptian philosophy, the Thinkers and Philosophers of Alexandria, Cyrenes, Carthage and Hippo (an era which included the great Euclid of geometry fame); the Cyrenaic School of Libya (the birth of Hedonism); Eratosthenes of the Alexandrian School (who measured the earth); Claudius Maximus of Carthage; and last but not least, Saint Augustine of Algeria.

Any student of philosophy and economic history would readily recognize most of the above-mentioned individuals. Their contributions shaped philosophical thought for many centuries and, indeed, some of their contributions have stood the test of time.

Professor G. M. James in his book *Stolen Legacy* (Sertima, 1993) goes as far as accusing Greek philosophers of having stolen African Egyptian ideas based on the Egyptian Mystery System. Those individuals accused of theft include Pythagoras, Zeno, Democritus, Socrates, Plato and Aristotle. James indicates that these individuals either traveled to Egypt or where taught by others who had journeyed to Egypt. We, however, realize that geographically contiguous lands interchange cultures; consequently, no one has a monopoly on any particular culture.

This study is not intended to cast aspersions, nor is it intended to point out inaccuracies in history. The primary focus is to evaluate the positions of selected black economists and to provide some insight into their theories and contributions.

The individuals selected for inclusion in this study all received formal training in economics. They are all to some degree contemporaries and have in one way or another made significant contributions to the field. On that basis, those selected include Sir W. Arthur Lewis, Kwame Nkrumah, Thomas Sowell, W. E. B. Du Bois, Walter Williams, Andrew Brimmer,

Clifton Wharton, Jr., Glenn Loury, William Darity, and Phyllis Ann Wallace. The order in which they appear is largely random.

The study borrows liberally from several sources, including books by the economists and biographical information from the following sources: *Contemporary Black Biography: Profiles from the International Black Community* edited by Barbara Carlisle Bigelow and L. Mpho Mabunda, *Great Economists Since Keynes: An Introduction to the Lives of 100 Modern Economists* by Mark Blaug, *The Evolution of Economic Thought* by Stanley L. Brue, and the *American Economics Review*, Vol. 84.

As each important individual is discussed, three areas will be considered. These are:

- The individual's background and influences.
- The individual's contributions.
- The validity and critical analysis of the individual's contributions.

It is our sincere hope that in this age of multiculturalism, this text can be used as a supplement in history of economic thought courses in the United States, as well as internationally. It could also very well be used as a primary text in a class on the history of black economic thought, and any number of black studies courses.

Series Editor's Preface

In the year 2000, *The Economist* magazine of London published a scandalous feature on what it called 'Africa: the Hopeless Continent'. This book, *A Critical Analysis of the Contributions of Notable Black Economists*, indirectly serves as a fitting rebuttal to the doomsday prophesy of *The Economist*. The magazine abandoned any pretence of balanced reporting by focusing exclusively on the crises that face Africans today without mentioning the immense human, intellectual, cultural and material resources that Africa is blessed with.

The naivety of the hopelessness of *The Economist* is again indirectly debunked by the fact that Professor Kojo Quartey courageously worked on this book in the year 2000 despite losing his beloved father and mentor the same year, proving that even in the valley of the shadow of death, Africans remain optimistic about the greatness of the continent.

Evidence of the amazing antiquity of the greatness of African economists comes in chapter two in the form of ancient scholars and theorists who provided instruction to Greek thinkers but unfortunately those Greeks and their modern followers failed to give credit to the African gurus that preceded them by thousands of years.

The question that this chapter indirectly poses is whether a continent that produced such intellectual giants can be dismissed by journalists who are intellectual nobodies as a hopeless continent? The answer in the whole book is an emphatic negative as the reader goes from page to page, from dazzling genius to awesome genius, male and female, Nobel Laureate specialist and social science generalists, academics and organic intellectuals, all descendants of a people who defiantly survived systematic genocidal attacks that lasted for more than five hundred years and are continuing in different guises today.

The book should serve as a good lesson for general readers who might be uninformed about the contributions of Africans to the important discipline of economics. For young scholars of African descent, the book should serve as a challenge. The reader should not see this book as a praise song or hero worship since the author uncovers controversies after controversies that invite the reader to evaluate the thinkers that are included in the book critically to see which of their ideas would serve the development of Africa today and which ideas would have to be modified or rejected to make room for new or more effective ideas even from black thinkers that are not included in the book. The fact that only one female economist of African descent and only one continental African man is included in this book should serve as an encouragement to other writers to continue the worthwhile excavation that Professor Quartey started here.

Biko Agozino, Associate Professor
Indiana University of Pennsylvania

Acknowledgements

I wish to express my sincere appreciation to all those individuals who aided me in making this study a success.

I wish to thank Dr. David Henson, president of Lincoln University; Dr. Arnold Parks, Lincoln University; Dr. Joseph Johnson, former president of Talladega College; Dr. Arthur Bacon and Ms. Althea Garret, Talladega College; and Ms. Audrey Simmons, Florida A&M University for their support and encouragement. In addition, special appreciation goes to Ms. Mary Bitter for her work on the first draft and to Ms. Rhonda Rose for her diligent work on the final draft.

Also, I owe a special gratitude to all those I have failed to mention by name. Finally, special thanks to my mother, Victoria Quartey, and my father, E. K. Quartey, for instilling in me the qualities of hard work and perseverance.

1 The Nature of Economics

What is economics? This is a question that many individuals have a difficult time answering. Indeed, even some professional economists tend to narrowly define economics. That being the case, how would one expect a young student to understand economics or aspire to become an economist? If one were to ask youngsters if they want to grow up to be an economist, how many of them would even understand the question?

More often than not, the concept of economics is linked to money and to various quantitative analyses. For the purpose of this book, economics is defined much more broadly to include the various areas of philosophy, social science and business, as well as mathematical and quantitative analyses. We begin by providing various definitions of economics to give the reader a better understanding of the nature of economics en route to understanding what it is that economists do and why certain individuals have been included in this book.

Definitions of Economics

Most, if not all, economics textbooks begin by defining economics. In that sense, this text is no different.

Michael Parkin defines economics simply as 'the science of choice,' the science that explains the choices we make and how those choices change as we cope with *scarcity* (Parkin, 1998).

Paul Samuelson and William Nordhaus define economics as 'the study of how society uses scarce resources to produce *valuable* commodities and distribute them among different people' (Samuelson and Nordhaus, 1998).

Karl Case and Ray Fair define economics as 'the study of how individuals and societies choose to use the scarce resources that nature and previous generations have provided' (Case and Fair, 1999).

Other definitions of economics include the following:

- The science or study of wealth (welfare) and its production, applicable either to the individual, the family, the state, or in the widest sense, the world (Hewins, 1910).

- Mainly concerned with...such human activities as are directed towards the production, appropriation, and application of the material means of satisfying human desires, so far as such means are capable of being exchanged.[1]
- The study of the allocation of scarce resources among unlimited and competing uses. It is the social science that deals with the ways in which men and societies seek to satisfy their material needs and desires, since the means at their disposal do not permit them to do so completely (Rees, 1968).

Yet other definitions involve the use of words such as production, distribution and consumption of goods and services.

The common theme in all of these definitions involves *scarcity* and *choices*. Simply put, economics deals with the choices we are forced to make because of scarcity, which arises from our inability to satisfy our unlimited wants.

That being said, everything we do in our daily lives involves economics to some degree; consequently, economics is a science, an art, a social science, and a field of business. Indeed, economics is imbued in art, music, finance, marketing, philosophy, physics, mathematics, etc. Perhaps Alfred Marshall put it best when he wrote that economics is a study of mankind in the ordinary business of life (Marshall, 1920).

What Do Economists Do?

Now that we understand the nature of economics, just what do economists do?

Essentially, economists are involved in numerous activities, including but not limited to the following:

- Study the behavior of labor, capital and other factors of production, and set their prices.
- Study the behavior of financial markets.
- Study the distribution of income.
- Study the roles of households, firms, and the government.

---

[1] Henry Sedgwick in *The New Palgrave: A Dictionary of Economics*, vol. 2, edited by John Eatwell, Murray Milgate, and Peter Newman (London: The Macmillan Press Limited, 1987), p. 59: reprinted from *Palgrave's Dictionary of Political Economy*, vol. 1, edited by Henry Higgs (London: Macmillan and Company Limited, 1926), p. 679.

- Study production distribution and consumption of goods and services.
- Study unemployment and price level changes.
- Study international trade and its impact on the economy.
- Study the growth of the economy and fluctuations in the business cycle.
- Study the impact of environmental factors on economic conditions.
- Study the impact of discrimination on the economy.
- Study the impact of poverty and inequality on the economy.
- Shape government policy.
- Provide advice on how individuals and businesses can be improved.
- Provide advice on how to make the world a better place in which to live.

The common thread, as stated earlier, has to do with scarcity. Economists deal with society's problems; they are social commentators, theorists, pragmatists and leaders. All the scholars included in this text were or are involved in one or more of these areas.

2 The Ancient African Scholars

It is impossible to discuss economic history without discussing philosophy and mathematics. The very history of economic thought begins with the ancient philosophers, such as Plato and Aristotle, and then goes on to deal with the Christian Economists. This text is no different; however, it focuses on the Black/African contribution. Prior to discussing the individual contributors, a general discussion and exposition of early contributors are provided. Indeed, economic thought has been shaped by philosophy and mathematics.

Giving Credit Where it is Due

Very little, if any, credit is given to Africans for their contributions. This is because African peoples have typically been viewed as inferior or lacking the wherewithal to produce anything of significance. As a consequence, there has been some attempt to disparage African achievement; thus, many great achievements have not been recognized. It is these very thoughts that gave rise to mercantilism, which led eventually to slavery and colonialism in Africa. This kind of thinking was further perpetuated by economists such as Friedrich List, who made the pronouncement that manufacturing could only develop in the temperate zone because only that climate would foster the necessary intellectual and physical effort (List, 1966). In essence, tropical areas such as Africa should supply raw materials in exchange for manufactured goods from Europe.

We examine the roles of several black economists in this book. Some of the individuals would readily be recognized as economists, yet others may not easily be viewed as such, perhaps because of a varied career or lack of any groundbreaking theory. This, however, does not preclude the individual from being considered as an economist.

The focus is on black economists because little, if any, significant work has been produced on black economists. Economic theory shapes every aspect of our lives, yet it seems so esoteric, abstract, and far-removed from our everyday lives.

4

A Review of the Literature on Ancient Greek Scholarship

This section sheds more light on Africa's contribution to economic theory and is intended to highlight the achievements of African scholars who have received little credit for their work, and to highlight the significant scholarly role that Africa played in the birth of economic science. It is not intended to claim the birth of economics for Africa, cast aspersion or demonize Europeans for depriving Africa of its history, or to fuel the flames or fan the fires of the Eurocentric versus Afrocentric debate.

Akomolafe correctly states that because Europe receives so much credit for numerous major achievements, Europeans have a great amount of racial pride (Akomolafe, 1998). By the same token, because Africans have been taught that they have made no or few contributions to humanity, they have much self-contempt. While Europe and Greece have celebrated their numerous achievements, Africans have lamented their 'unachievements.'

G. M. James, in his classic work *Stolen Legacy*, states that Greek philosophy was stolen from Egyptian philosophy (Akomolafe, 1998). To prove this point, he describes the Egyptian Mystery System secret order. This system, he claims, was unavailable to outsiders and was only developed when Alexander invaded Egypt and plundered the temples and libraries. He states that it was based upon those books that Aristotle built many of his theories. Pythagoras was a student in Egypt for many years, and Plato and Aristotle, in essence, violated the teachings of the Mystery System by writing books about what they had learned.

Professor Lefkowitz of Wellesley College attempts to put to rest some of these Afrocentric claims in her book *Not Out of Africa: How Afrocentrism Became an Excuse to Teach Myth as History* (Lefkowitz, 1992). In this book she states that all the claims made by the 'Afrocentrists' are without merit. She marshals evidence against the claims of scholars such as James, Diop, Ben-Jochanon and Bernal. She is a bit too quick, however, in her dismissal of a possible conspiracy to discredit African achievements.

This treatise is in no way meant to debunk or cast aspersion on any group or individual. It is intended to add to the literature by providing factual information on the contributions of African scholars. In that sense, the intention is not to fuel the Afrocentric vs. Eurocentric debate that has raged for years. While there are merits to both sides of the debate, unfortunately, like most debates, there is usually no resolution.

There are no attempts here to demonize, disparage or discredit any group. It is hoped that the information provided will uplift and spur a new generation of youth and scholars alike to view more positively the contributions of African scholarship and provide some positive role models for a new generation of youth. We seek to bring recognition and credit where it is due.

Several so-called 'Afrocentric' writers have dealt with the issue of Black/African scholarship. Invariably, all of these scholars seem to cast aspersions on the so-called 'Eurocentric' model. It is noteworthy to recount some of this debate at this point.

One of the earliest 'Afrocentric' writers was Marcus Garvey, the founder of the Universal Negro Improvement Association. Garvey was born in Jamaica, under British colonial rule. After emancipation from slavery in the United States, blacks were attempting to establish an identity for themselves. Slavery had dehumanized and deprecated the black race, and colonialism continued to ravage them. Garvey was one of the earliest black champions. He viewed history as a subject to further enhance the emancipation of a downtrodden people who had been stripped of all human dignity. He sought to reclaim the positive aspects of black history in an effort to instill confidence in a people who had essentially lost faith in themselves. In his essay *Who and What is a Negro*, published in 'Philosophy and Opinion' (Garvey and Garvey, 1923), Garvey wrote:

> The white world has always tried to rob and discredit us of our history....Every Student of history, of impartial mind, knows that the Negro once ruled the world, when white men were savages and barbarians living in caves; that thousands of Negro professors at that time taught in the universities in Alexandria, then the seat of learning; that ancient Egypt gave the world civilization and that Greece and Rome have robbed Egypt of her arts and letters, and taken all the credit to themselves.

This sort of thinking has survived Garvey, and other more research-oriented scholars besides James have taken on the fight.

Yet another scholar who adds fuel to the flames is the Senegalese historian Cheikh Anta Diop. In *The African Origin of Civilization* (Diop, 1967), Diop claimed that Europeans have consistently falsified evidence that suggests that the Egyptians were black-skinned. He traces Egyptian influence on Greece back to prehistoric times, claiming that Cecrops (a half-snake/half-man whom the Athenians themselves regarded as indigenous) came to Attica from Egypt, and Danaus (who, according to the Greeks, was of Greek descent) taught the Greeks agriculture and metallurgy. According to Diop, Greek mythology reflects the resentment of the Indo-Europeans against this cultural domination.

Other Afrocentric scholars, such as Yosef ben-Jochanan in *Africa: Mother of Western Civilization*, insinuate that Aristotle came to Egypt with Alexander the Great and sacked and looted the Egyptian temples with him (Lefkowitz, 1992). There is no evidence to support this claim.

Other Afrocentrists who have made contributions to the literature include Henry Louis Gates, Molefekete Asante, Leonard Jeffries, Lerone Bennett, Jr., Ali Mazuri, and one of the most controversial, Martin Bernal, author of the book *Black Athena: The Afroasiatic Roots of Classical Civilization* (Bernal, 1987). Bernal, a professor at Cornell has written one of the more controversial texts to date. In his book, Bernal argues that linguistic, technological and intellectual contributions of Africans played an important role in the development of Greek civilization. He uses information derived from writings by Herodotus, Plato and Aristotle, among others, to buttress his claims.

This sort of rhetoric, while it raises important issues, tends to demonize groups and not synthesize the scholarship. We avoid that in this section, realizing full well that, historically, various cultures have impacted each other. This is no different for Greek, Egyptian and other cultures with geographical proximity.

We now turn to specific information on African contributions.

Philosophers, Mathematicians, and Theologians (Scholastics)[2]

It is impossible to discuss economic history without discussing philosophy, mathematics and early Christian thought. The history of economic thought begins with the ancient philosophers, such as Plato and Aristotle, and then goes on to deal with the Christian Economists. This study is no different; however, it focuses on the Black/African contribution. Indeed, economic thought has been shaped by philosophy, mathematics and theology.

This section chronicles the contributions of notable African scholars. Since economics did not exist as a science in that period, the individuals in this section are mostly scientists, philosophers, mathematicians and theologians. Geographically, the focus is on Egypt, primarily Alexandria, Libya, Algeria and Ethiopia.

The section is divided into three parts, focusing on the philosophers, mathematicians and theologians/scholastics. As one begins to name names and give credit, it is easy to overlook some noteworthy individuals.

---

[2] All information in this section is from the Columbia, Compton and Catholic Encyclopedias online.

However, careful research has ensured that the most notable have been included. Every scholar listed in this section was African born – in Egypt, Ethiopia, Algeria, Carthage or elsewhere. While it is difficult to determine the exact color of these individuals, it must be noted that that is not our primary preoccupation. Our purpose here is to simply indicate their scholarly contributions. Some of the names we will see are readily recognizable (Euclid, St. Augustine), while others are only known in esoteric circles (Hypathia, Athanasius), and yet still others are obscure (Moses the Black, St. Didymus). Most are theologians or scholastics who contributed to early Christian thought.

We provide a brief description of each of these individuals, beginning with biographical information and scholarly contributions; with a focus on those contributions that are long-lasting. To the extent that the individuals made any economic pronouncements, such information will be provided.

The Philosophers

Theodorus (465-398 B.C.)

Theodorus of Cyrene was a pupil of Pythagoras and Plato. He authored works in mathematics and distinguished himself in astronomy, music and other subjects. He was a member of the society of Pythagoras and a major figure in the Cyrenaic School of moral philosophy. He believed that pleasures and pains are necessities for happiness.

He made noteworthy contributions to the development of irrational numbers. His results, Plato wrote, inspired Theaetetus and Socrates to make some generalizations concerning square roots. This alone is sufficient evidence that his contributions in mathematics are valid, useful and long-lasting. His influence is important also in the area of philosophy. As a member of the Cyrenaic School, he was instrumental in propounding the theory that influenced the Benthamites and their pleasure pain principle.

Aristippus (c. 435-c. 360 B.C.)

Aristippus was born in Cyrene and later traveled to Syracuse where he taught rhetoric. He then went to Athens where he became a student of Socrates. Aristippus founded the Cyrenaic School, which believed that all human sensations are reducible to the two emotions of pleasure and pain. Pleasure is considered the highest good and, thus, most individuals in a quest for happiness seek pleasure and avoid pain.

The Cyrenaic School has survived in principle for centuries. Apart from giving birth to Hedonism, it may arguably be viewed as a precursor of the Classical School's 'self-interested motive tenet.' The Cyrenaic School rivaled the Socratic School. It gave rise to the psychological theory that pleasure motivates human actions. Many, including Locke, Hume, Bentham, Hobbes, and the great economist, John Stuart Mill, have espoused the Hedonistic philosophy.

Arete of Cyrene

Arete was the daughter of Aristippus, founder of the Cyrenaic School. After his death, he was succeeded by Arete who taught philosophy for 30 years, wrote 40 books, and trained over 100 philosophers. She helped the Cyrenaic School survive.

The Mathematicians

Euclid (c. 300 B.C.-?)

Euclid was the prominent mathematician of his time and, arguably, until this day. He was born in Alexandria, Egypt. He is the author of one of the most successful mathematics texts ever. He is considered the father of geometry and authored the text *Elements*. This text dealt with arithmetic, space and geometry. Euclid studied and lived in Alexandria and opened a mathematics school there. Some claim that he was a Greek who traveled to Egypt. While this is entirely possible, there is no evidence to support it. Euclid's *Elements* has stood the test of time and has been translated, revised and recopied.

His theories have proven their validity and relevance, as we continue to use them in mathematics and economics, among other areas, to this day.

Eratosthenes (c. 276-194 B.C.)

Eratosthenes was born in Cyrene and died in Alexandria, yet numerous writings claim he was 'Greek.' He was a scientist, poet and mathematician, and was the first man known to have calculated the earth's circumference. He became director of the library in Alexandria. He also worked on a calendar that included leap years.

His contributions are valid and relevant to this day, especially in reference to his attempt to calculate the earth's circumference, calendar including leap years, and the famous sieve of Eratosthenes, which calculates prime numbers.

Hypathia

Born in Alexandria, Hypathia was the leading female mathematician of her time. She rose to become the head of the Platonic School. She taught geometry, mathematics, philosophy and astronomy, and was renowned throughout the region. Her contributions, although ignored for 1500 years, are still valid and relevant. She wrote on the division of cones into different parts by a plane, the idea of hyperbolas, parabolas and ellipses. Her contributions to early mathematics cannot be belied.

The Theologians

The individuals covered in this section have, in most instances, been canonized by the church. Their writings, although philosophical in nature, were religiously oriented.

Although clearly African, there is constant reference to their philosophies as 'Greek philosophy.'

St. Gregory the Wonderwork (A.D. 203-?)

Not to be confused with any of the other Gregories, he was born in Neocaesaria and given the name Theodore. He was educated in Alexandria as a pupil of Origen. He later became Bishop of Caesarea. He was renowned for converting many pagans to Christianity. He was a magnificent writer who wrote many homilies, most of which focused on the Word of God.

St. Moses the Black (Ethiopian)

Sometimes called Moses the Ethiopian, he was a slave and former criminal who converted to Christianity.

Origen (c. A.D. 185-c. 254)

He was born in Alexandria and was a student of Clement. He taught in Alexandria for almost 30 years, where he composed many treatises and critical works. He founded a school of literature, philosophy and theology in Caesarea. He is considered the most accomplished Biblical scholar of the early church. He is also given credit as a father of the allegorical method of scriptural interpretation.

He was a voluminous writer who combined philosophy and Christianity. He developed the concept of Christ as the Incarnate Word.

Athanasius (c. A.D. 295-373)

Athanasius was born and educated in Alexandria. In A.D. 319 he was ordained a deacon by Alexander. He became bishop of Alexandria after the death of Alexander. Because of disagreements with the church, he was exiled on several occasions.

His works have proven valid and long-lasting because of his emphasis on faith over religion.

Clement of Alexandria (A.D. 150?-215)

He was the principle exponent of the Alexandrian School of Theology. He received his early education in Athens. He traveled widely. His works relate Christianity to Greek philosophy and speak to the concept of wealth and salvation. His last extant work is a treatise on Mark 10:17-31 entitled *Who is the Rich Man That is Saved?* His contributions are relevant to the extent that issues such as wealth and religion are still being discussed today.

St. Augustine of Hippo (A.D. 354-430)

Augustine was born in Algeria. He attended the University of Carthage at age 16. He taught rhetoric in Carthage and then moved to Rome and Milan. In Milan, he was baptized as a Christian. He eventually returned to Algeria where he was ordained a priest and consecrated a bishop.

His ideas were set forth in his books *Confessions* and *City of God*. His writings gave strong support to the theory that the church was above the state. His contributions are valid because his writings on communal life are the basis for the 'Rule of St. Augustine,' which is espoused by many religious orders.   He may be regarded as the first of the Christian Economists.

Other noteworthy African scholars of lesser note include the following:

St. Macarius the Egyptian (or Elder):   Founder of a monastic community who wrote over fifty homilies.

St. Macarius the Alexandrian: A hermit monk generally credited with composing a rule for monks.

Dionysus of Alexandria: Eminent bishop of the third century.

Heraclas: Bishop of Alexandria from A.D. 231-232.   Considered very knowledgeable about philosophy.

Didymus the Blind: Head of the Catechetical School of Alexandria. Wrote numerous commentaries on the Bible.

St. Anthony: An Egyptian hermit who was the first Christian monk. He was a wealthy young man who sold all he had and gave to the poor, thus, practicing the extremist form of Christian economics. He is considered the father of all monks.

Pantaenus: He headed the Catechetical School of Alexandria and was one of the first to cite philosophy as an aid to theology.

St. Isidore of Petusium: Born in Alexandria, he eventually became a monk and wrote voluminously on religion and discipline.

St. Demetrius: He is the first Alexandrian bishop of whom anything is known (A.D. 188-231).

Celcus the Platonist: He attacked Christianity and its tenets.

Cyprian of Carthage: This bishop of Carthage wrote several books, which are still extant.

The following individuals are also of note: Arius (Libyan), Eusebius (Alexandrian), St. Rufinus (at least three African individuals by this name), St. Cyril of Alexandria, and Dioscrus.

This list of ancient scholars is by no means exhaustive. There may be some greater or lesser scholars who have been omitted. The individuals identified, however, are representative of ancient African scholarship.

Since the tradition of many other areas of the African continent was oral, little is known about the scholarship in those parts. The great contributions of the sub-Saharan Africans cannot be belied. There were undoubtedly some significant contributions made by the kingdoms of Ghana, Mali, Songhay and other sub-Saharan empires.

Now it is time to turn to the more contemporary scholars.

3 William Edward Burghardt Du Bois – The Multi-disciplinary Scholar (1868-1963)

We begin with W. E. B. Du Bois (pronounced Duboyce) because he is without a doubt the most well known scholar included in this text. He is noted as one of the foremost multi-disciplinary and prolific scholars of the twentieth century. In this author's view, he was the first major black economist of the modern era.

Du Bois, due to his multi-disciplinary training, has not been considered an economist. Indeed, this is the first study that unequivocally grants him this status. He was a prolific writer who received training in economics (obtaining higher degrees in agricultural economics) and propounded economic theories. Du Bois was a controversial scholar who was also a historian, sociologist, political activist, author and educator. Due to his varied background, he is more commonly claimed by the sociologists and historians. This study casts his contributions in an economic context, although he was not a pure theorist. He was a founder of the Niagara Movement and the NAACP, and wrote numerous books.

Our discussion of Du Bois will proceed as follows. First we look at his biographical background, educational background, and influences. We then consider his ideas as they relate to the controversies in which he was involved. Finally, we examine his many writings and speeches to cull his economic ideas and contributions and critically assess their validity in today's world.

On Du Bois' hundredth birthday (five years after his death), Dr. Martin Luther King, Jr. delivered the address honoring Du Bois at Carnegie Hall. This was Dr. King's last major address before his assassination. Dr. King recognized Du Bois as an 'Intellectual giant,...tireless explorer and gifted discoverer of social truth' (Foner, 1970). Despite the many praises heaped upon Dr. Bois posthumously, he received scant recognition while living, and was in many instances ostracized and vilified. He was exiled before his death.

Du Bois is an African-American icon. He was a multi-talented and multi-disciplinary scholar who lived for almost a century. Du Bois has been hailed as a sociologist, historian, philosopher, anthropologist, political scientist, educator and journalist, but hardly ever has he been recognized as an economist.

According to John Milton Cooper, Du Bois was a genius who 'ranks with Frederick Douglass, Booker T. Washington, and Martin Luther King, Jr. as one of the four greatest blacks in history' (Marable, 1986). He has been hailed as the 'Father of Pan-Africanism,' a central theoretician of African independence, and the major social scientist of his time. Du Bois has also been recognized as the founder of black studies.

This study was undertaken to examine the life's work of Du Bois primarily in the field of economics. While hardly ever recognized as an economist, Du Bois was an economist in the truest sense of the word. He received formal training in economics and completed doctoral work in the area at the University of Berlin.

His Life and Times

Du Bois was born on February 23, 1868 in Great Barrington, Massachusetts. The family patriarch, Tom, was born in West Africa and brought as a slave to the region by a Dutch family. His father, Alfred, was born in Haiti and served as a private in the Union army. He left when William was a year old. His mother, Mary, worked intermittently as a maid and raised William on her own. While growing up in Great Barrington, he experienced little racism. While his family was less affluent than those of his peers, he observed they were not as poor as the Irish working class. He recalled a pleasant childhood (Du Bois, 1968).

Du Bois enrolled in local public school where he outdid most of his classmates intellectually. While in high school he worked odd jobs, including splitting wood, shoveling coal and mowing lawns. He also served briefly as co-editor of the school's newspaper, the *Howler*, and was Great Barrington correspondent to the *Springfield Republican* and local correspondent to the *Globe*, an African-American weekly. He took great interest in politics, attending town meetings, church, etc. By age 16 he had come to the conclusion that black Americans could not exercise their full democratic rights unless they organized themselves within a race-conscious bloc; group cooperation was essential to advance democratic reforms. While in high school he broadened his horizons by studying Greek and Latin. In 1884, the year of the partition of Africa, Du Bois graduated from high school with high honors as the valedictorian and delivered an oration on abolitionist and socialist leader Wendell Phillips. He was the first black graduate in the school's history (Marable, 1986).

After the sudden death of Du Bois' mother in 1883, Reverend C. C. Pointer and others secured enough funds for him to attend Fisk University in Nashville, Tennessee in 1885. At Fisk, Du Bois studied a variety of subjects, including German, history, French, botany, rhetoric and calculus. He was also editor of the *Fisk Herald* and taught school during the summer in the Tennessee countryside. This experience opened his eyes to the plight of the southern Negro. He began to identify more with the struggle. In a *Fisk Herald* editorial of 1888, Du Bois is quoted as dedicating himself 'toward a life that shall be an honor to the Race.' Upon graduation from Fisk, Du Bois raised funds to study at Harvard by joining other glee club members to work as bus boys at a resort in Minnesota (Du Bois, 1968).

Du Bois graduated from Fisk in 1888. He selected as his commencement address the subject of Bismarck. Du Bois was admitted to Harvard in 1888 as a junior and was awarded $250 from the Price-Greenleaf Fund. At Harvard, Du Bois studied economics, geology, qualitative analysis, French, German, philosophy and logic. Du Bois was not allowed to join the Harvard Glee Club because of his color. In 1889 he won a Matthews Scholarship for placing second in the Boylston Prizes in oratory. In 1890 Du Bois graduated and was selected to deliver one of the commencement addresses. His topic was Jefferson Davis, and he received critical acclaim for his delivery (Marable, 1986).

In 1890 Du Bois won the H. B. Rogers Memorial Fellowship in Political Science to pursue his masters at Harvard. Despite his scholastic abilities, Du Bois was not permitted to join the Graduates Club, solely on racial grounds. In 1892 he received his master of arts degree in history (Marable, 1986).

Du Bois had long harbored intentions of studying overseas, so in 1892 he succeeded in winning a Slater Fund for the Education of Negroes scholarship to study at Friedreich Wilhelm University in Berlin. He studied history and economics under Gustav Schmoller, Rudolph von Gneist, Adolf Wagner and Max Weber. Here he experienced no racism, but did see anti-Semitism. He traveled around Europe and began to perceive the broader class dimensions of racial oppression. Upon completing his course work and his dissertation in the area of agricultural economics (plantation economics in the South), Du Bois was unable to receive his doctorate because he had attended classes for only three semesters, not the minimum five. Thus, the faculty refused to give him an oral examination. Although wishing to remain another year, his Slater Fund was not renewed. He returned to the United States in 1892 and obtained a position at Wilberforce University in Ohio, teaching Greek and Latin. In 1895 he received his Ph.D. in history from Harvard. He was the first black to receive a Ph.D. in any field from Harvard (McKissack and McKissack, 1990).

Du Bois left Wilberforce in 1896 to take the position of assistant instructor of sociology at the University of Pennsylvania. He taught no classes, but was responsible for studying the conditions of Negroes in Philadelphia. This led to his text *The Philadelphia Negro: A Special Study.* Du Bois spent the summer of 1897 studying the black population in Farmville, Virginia. In the same year he obtained a position as professor of economics and history at Atlanta University. He studied the black population in Georgia and Alabama and published articles on the subject. Du Bois initiated a series of conferences focusing on the plight of the Negro. During this period he established the foundations for black sociology and became the leading social scientist on black America (Marable, 1986).

In 1900 Du Bois served as secretary of the first Pan-African Conference in London, England. He was involved in writing numerous articles and books and in 1903 published his classic *The Souls of Black Folk.* In 1905 he became the main founder and secretary of the Niagara movement. In 1907 he founded and edited *The Horizon,* a Washington, DC monthly. He helped found the NAACP in 1910 and served as a member of the board, director of publicity and research, and editor of its journal, the *Crisis.* During his years as editor he struggled with the board over control of the *Crisis.* He began to become more politically involved in domestic affairs. He met with Max Weber in 1904 and had one of his essays included in a journal edited by Weber. He began to build an international reputation. In 1911 Du Bois was invited to participate in the first Universal Races Congress in London. Beginning to feel even more strongly that socialism was less deleterious to blacks, he joined the socialist party in 1911. By 1912 he had become disenchanted with the party and resigned. He became a leading political activist, leading boycotts and organizing movements (Du Bois, 1968).

By 1919 the new Pan-African movement was afoot and Du Bois was a major organizer. In 1920 he received the NAACP Spingarn Award for his dedication to its cause. In 1921 and 1923 Du Bois chaired the second and third Pan-African Congresses in London, Brussels and Paris, and London, Paris and Lisbon, respectively. Du Bois was appointed by President Calvin Coolidge as special minister and 'envoy extraordinary' for the United States at the inauguration of President Charles D. B. King of Liberia in 1923 (Du Bois, 1985). He traveled for six weeks in the Soviet Union and came to believe that the Soviet system was more equitable in terms of race than that of the United States. Du Bois was involved in the Harlem Renaissance, contributing his book *Dark Princess: A Romance* and founding black theater (the KRIGWA players) in Harlem (Marable, 1986).

Du Bois, after unsuccessfully attempting to democratize the NAACP by introducing economic cooperatives as a step toward black self-sufficiency, resigned in 1936 from the NAACP and *Crisis*, but still remained on its board. He returned to Atlanta University to serve as professor and chairman of the Department of Sociology. In 1935 he published *Black Reconstruction*, which analyzed the role of the Negro in reconstruction. He founded and edited *Phylon*, a quarterly publication. Du Bois traveled extensively and served in 1945 with Mary McLeod Bethune and Walter White as NAACP representatives to the founding of the United Nations. At this conference he sought in vain to persuade the delegation to adopt an anti-colonial position. During the same year he presided at the Fifth Pan-African Congress in Manchester, England. In 1948 Du Bois resigned from the NAACP board as a result of his opposition to the cold war policies of the United States (Marable, 1986).

During the 1950s, while in his 80s, Du Bois did not rest on his laurels. He continued to be productive. In 1950 he ran for the United States Senate in New York on the American Labor Party ticket. He received 210,000 votes, much more than he had anticipated, but was still unsuccessful. Moving more in the communist direction, Du Bois was indicted in 1950-51 under the McCormick Act as an 'unregistered foreign agent.' He was arrested and tried, but was acquitted. Du Bois traveled around the world again with visits to China and the U.S.S.R. In 1961 Du Bois finally joined the United States Communist party. Facing continued pressure in the United States because of his communist affiliation, Du Bois moved to Ghana at the request of President Kwame Nkrumah to edit the *Encyclopedia Africana*. He became a Ghanaian citizen in 1963 and died on August 27, 1963, the day of the great march on Washington, DC. Du Bois was given a state funeral and buried in Accra, Ghana (Marable, 1986).

The Controversies and Conflicts

Many scholars of African American history are no doubt familiar with Du Bois' famous 'debates' with Booker T. Washington and the Tuskegee

Machine. As a radical scholar, the controversies surrounding him were many. Apart from the debates with Booker T. Washington, there were conflicts with Marcus Garvey, the United States government, the leaders of the NAACP, and other black scholars. Du Bois' lifetime was full of controversies. He feuded with his cohorts at the NAACP, most notably Villard and White, with Florence M. Read, president of Atlanta's Spelman College, and with several others. Du Bois even feuded with the United States government when he was indicted under the McCormick Act as an 'unregistered foreign agent.' The most notable controversies, however, were with the two greatest black figures of those times, Booker T. Washington and Marcus Garvey.

Du Bois versus Booker T. Washington

The most famous and widely publicized conflict involved Du Bois' debates with the most powerful black man during the earliest part of the twentieth century, Booker T. Washington. Washington, educated at Hampton Institute, eventually founded and became the principal of Tuskegee Institute. Du Bois had great admiration and respect for Washington and actually worked at Tuskegee during the summer of 1903. Although reluctant to criticize Washington, Du Bois was at such odds with his philosophy that he felt compelled to do so in his classic *The Souls of Black Folk* (Du Bois, 1989).

So powerful was Booker T. Washington in those days that most government appointments for blacks were at his behest. Washington was in favor of industrial training for blacks. Du Bois stated that Washington represented 'the old attitude of adjustment and submission.'

Du Bois' view was that of the Talented Tenth uplifting the masses. He favored education in the arts and sciences for blacks and was in favor of universal suffrage. Du Bois' idea of the Talented Tenth, to Washington, was an indication of his refusal to identify with the masses. According to the Tuskegee Machine, he was an elitist who could not identify with most blacks. According to Du Bois, the Tuskegee Machine was accommodationist in that they sought to win the favors of the whites in order to serve their own selfish purpose (Du Bois, 1989).

While Washington was a mobilizer, natural leader and shrewd tactician, Du Bois was a scholar, researcher and social critic. He did not have the following of Washington and, without a doubt, Washington was the most powerful Negro in that era. At a reconciliation meeting in 1904 involving Du Bois and Washington, Du Bois made it clear that he was not against industrial education, but was against Washington's 'attacks upon higher training and upon his general attitude of belittling the race and not putting enough stress upon voting.' After the meeting, an executive committee consisting of Du Bois, Washington and H. M. Browne, a Washington supporter, was appointed to carry out further action. However, further action was forestalled due to Washington's control. Du Bois accused Washington of 'bribery and intimidation' but was unable to provide concrete proof; consequently, Du Bois' reputation was marred (Marable, 1986).

Due to Washington's enormous power and control of the black press, Du Bois led the creation of a militant civil rights organization, the Niagara Movement, in order to neutralize Washington. Among its objectives were 'freedom of speech and criticism,' 'manhood suffrage,' 'the abolition of caste distinctions based simply on race or color,' and 'the recognition of the principle of human brotherhood as a practical present creed.' Du Bois was elected as the general secretary, which led to the formation of the NAACP in 1910. All of the national elected officers were white, with the exception of Du Bois, who served as director of publicity and research. Du Bois created the journal *Crisis*, which would be the voice of the NAACP for many years. Due especially to opposition from the NAACP, Washington's power was soon curtailed until his death in 1915 (Marable, 1986).

In comparing Du Bois and Washington, William H. Ferris noted the following: 'Du Bois is gifted with a more powerful intellect than Washington, is a more uncompromising idealist, and is a more brilliant writer. But Washington is a more magnetic speaker and more astute politician, a greater humorist, and less of an aristocrat' (Marable, 1986).

After Washington's death, Du Bois wrote the following obituary (Marable, 1986):

> He was the greatest Negro leader since Frederick Douglass....Of the good that he accomplished there can be no doubt. He directed the attention of the Negro race in America to the pressing necessity of economic development, he emphasized technical education and he did much to pave the way for interracial understanding....On the other hand, in stern justice, we must lay on the soul of this man, a heavy responsibility for the consummation of Negro disfranchisement, the decline of the Negro college and public school and the firmer establishment of color caste.

Du Bois versus Marcus Garvey

> In his fifty-five years, Du Bois personally has made a success of nothing. In all his journalistic, personal and other business efforts he has failed, and were it not for [his white associates], Du Bois, no doubt, would be eating his pork chops

from the counter of the cheapest restaurant in Harlem like many other Negro graduates of Harvard and Fisk.

Marcus Garvey, 1923 (Marable, 1986)

Marcus Garvey is, without doubt, the most dangerous enemy of the Negro race in America and in the world. He is either a lunatic or a traitor...this open ally of the Ku Klux Klan should be locked up or sent home.

W. E. B. Du Bois, 1927 (Marable, 1986)

Perhaps a more bitter feud than that with Washington involved the polemics with the most powerful black leader after Washington's death, Marcus Garvey. Garvey was born in Jamaica in 1887 and worked as a printer and journalist in the Caribbean, Central America and England. In 1914 Garvey founded the Universal Negro Improvement Association (UNIA). He was influenced by the philosophy of Booker T. Washington. To many poor and working class blacks, the UNIA was a viable alternative to the NAACP. Garvey was in favor of black nationalism, Pan-Africanism, and racial pride. He founded a shipping company, The Black Star Line. He was a dynamic speaker and leader, yet egocentric. Du Bois viewed Garvey as a 'demagogue,' yet 'an extraordinary leader of men.' Garvey viewed Du Bois as an 'elitist sell-out.' Contrary to popular belief, Du Bois did not have any major problems with Garvey's philosophy, observing that Garvey's economic strategy was 'perfectly feasible.' Du Bois stated, 'What he is trying to say and do is this. American Negroes can, by accumulating and monitoring their own capital, organize industry, join the black centers of the south Atlantic by commercial enterprise and in this way ultimately redeem Africa as a fit and free home for black men. This is true' (Marable, 1986).

As Garveyism grew, Du Bois' Pan-African movement began to decline and the Ku Klux Klan coincidentally began to grow. Garvey made conciliatory moves toward the group and formed alliances with other white supremacist groups, declaring that they were 'better friends of the race' than the NAACP because of their 'honesty of purpose toward the Negro.' This was the basis of the polemics between these two great men. This angered Du Bois and soon the two resorted to personal attacks. Du Bois began receiving death threats from Garveyites. It was such a feud that A. Phillip Randolph described it as the 'Heavyweight Championship Bout for Afro-American-West Indian Belt, Between Battling Du Bois and Kid Garvey' (McKissack and McKissack, 1990). Du Bois nonetheless took no active role in the anti-Garvey movement. Garvey was imprisoned for fraud in 1925, his company went bankrupt, and he was pardoned and deported to Jamaica in 1927. In

1944 Du Bois solicited the aid of Garvey's widow to organize the fifth Pan-African Congress.

Influences

Du Bois was a man of many talents. We must uncover his influences in order to gain a better understanding of this most intricate and complex genius. Like all great men, no one develops in a vacuum. Du Bois was no different. He had numerous influences from his childhood until his death at age 95.

Du Bois has been described as a cultural pluralist and Calvinist early in his career, and as a radical democrat all his life. Perhaps to some extent he was all of that. He was intolerant of racial discrimination and had a good Christian upbringing. It was the Calvinist dogma of his little New England town that shaped his early thoughts. Undoubtedly, his first influence was his mother. She instilled in him the values of hard work and thrift. She believed that education was the key to success, while wealth was the result of commitment, hard work and personal sacrifice (McKissack and McKissack, 1990).

Some of Du Bois' earliest influences were Frank Hosman, his high school principal, Reverend E. Sander, pastor of the Congregational Church, and Reverend C. C. Pointer, who were responsible for sending him to Fisk. At Fisk, Du Bois' Calvinist training soon changed. One of his major influences was Adam Spence, professor of classics, who guided him through the classics. Other influences at Fisk included Erastus Cravath, the president, Tom Calloway, business manager for the *Herald*, and Frederick A. Chase, physical science instructor.

Several professors at Harvard impacted Du Bois' thought immensely. They include George Santayana, under whom he studied French and German philosophy, and William James, who taught him logic. Albert Bushnell Hart, who taught a political history course, instilled in the young man 'an appreciation for scholarly documentation, rigorous research, and literary restraint.' Adam Sherman Hill influenced his prose style. James was a pragmatist who believed that truth was in action; if you act on it, it works. The pragmatist philosophy of James left an indelible mark on the young man's thoughts. Another influence was Josiah Royce, a speculative philosophy professor. Du Bois says about these influences (Foner, 1970):

> The Harvard of 1888 was an extraordinary aggregation of great men. Not often if ever since that day have so many distinguished teachers been together in one

place and at one time. There was William James, the psychologist; Palmer in Ethics; Royce and Santayana in philosophy; Shaler in geology; and Hart in history. The president was the cold, precise but exceedingly efficient Charles William Eliot and there were a dozen lesser lights. By extraordinary good fortune I was thrown into contact with most of these men. I was repeatedly a guest in the house of William James; of all teachers, he was my closest friend. I was a member of the philosophical club, I talked often with Royce and Shaler, I sat alone in an upper room and read Kant's *Critique* with Santayana; I became one of Hart's favorite pupils and was afterwards guided by him through my graduate course and started on my work in Germany. It was an extraordinary opportunity for a young man and I think I realized it. I evolved habits of work rather different from those of most of the other students.

Josephine St. Pierre Ruffin, a national leader of the black women's club and editor of the *Boston Courant*, which published several of Du Bois' papers, undoubtedly influenced his views on women's suffrage. He no longer had Calvinistic views, and had begun to identify with the larger black community.

Schmoller and The German Historical School

In Germany, Du Bois' economic ideas began to take shape. The most influential individual at this stage was most likely the 'professor maker' himself, Gustav Schmoller. Under Schmoller, Du Bois conducted research on patterns of plantation economics and peonage in the United States South. Schmoller was the leader of the younger German Historical School, which had as its basis inductive/historical reasoning as opposed to deductive theorizing. This method placed emphasis on advocating conservative reform and the accumulation of historical and descriptive factual materials, which is what Du Bois did in most of his studies.

The German Historical School had four basic tenets: (1) evaluation approach to economics, (2) emphasis on the positive role of government, (3) inductive/historical approach, and (4) advocacy of conservative reform (Brue, 1994).

The leading figure of the younger historical school was Gustav Schmoller, who was Du Bois' professor at Berlin. Schmoller contended that the accumulation of historical and descriptive factual materials was to come prior to and was more important than deductive theorizing. He engaged in the famous battle of methods (methodenstreit) with Carl Menger. This clash of methods involved a debate as to whether inductive or deductive thinking was better. According to Schumpeter, the controversy was pointless since the methods complement each other (Schumpeter, 1981). Schmoller believed in ethical value judgments. He further stated that equitable distribution of income would lead to social reform. He continually emphasized historical study. Policies were to be based on empirical evidence. He and his followers have been described by some not as economists, but as historically minded sociologists. Du Bois was that, but he was even more. Schmoller also believed in protectionism. There was a failure on the part of the Germans to make lasting contributions to economics. Their nationalism, however, led to greater support of the Nazi philosophy.

Other influences while in Germany included Max Weber, another economist who belonged to the same school, and Adolph Wagner, who taught Du Bois political economy.

Other Influences

Two of the major black intellectuals who influenced Du Bois were Edward Wilmot Blyden and Alexander Crummell. Blyden, who had migrated to Liberia, served as its secretary of state and ambassador to Great Britain and later became president of Liberia College. He lectured and promoted research in African history and culture. His major premise was that black people were distinct because of their spirituality and rejection of materialism. Du Bois listened to some of his lectures and read his writings (Marable, 1986).

Crummell was born a free black in New York City. He had been educated in England and moved to Liberia in 1853. Together with Blyden, he established a literary society for Liberian intellectuals. He was an Episcopal minister whose ideology centered on racial solidarity and black pride. Du Bois greatly admired Crummell and he became Du Bois' 'spiritual father.' To Du Bois, he was the personification of all that black intellectuals should be. Crummell's ideas shaped much of Du Bois' thoughts (Du Bois, 1989).

Other influences included William Monroe Trotter, editor of the *Boston Guardian*, who led the initial charge against Booker T. Washington. It was his charge that spurred Du Bois to oppose Washington. Also, George Padmore was influential in building Du Bois' Pan-African program. Du Bois acquainted himself with the writings of socialists and radical liberals, such as Jack London, John Spargo and Henry George. He did not read Marx and Engels, and made observations independent of Lenin. William Walling, Charles Russell and Upton Sinclair influenced Du Bois with their social patriotism (Marable, 1986).

Writings and Scholarship

While Du Bois believed that work and wealth would uplift the disadvantaged, he believed that knowledge and culture were greater resources for the disadvantaged. He believed education was the key to economic development.

Du Bois was one of the most prolific writers to have ever lived. He delivered numerous speeches, wrote poems, essays, newspaper and journal articles, and much, much more. Following is an overview of his major writings.

Du Bois' first publication was 'The Suppression of the African Slave, Trade to the United States of America 1638-1870,' which was his doctoral dissertation. In this study he traces the history of the slave trade, with the bulk of the text examining the political and legal dimensions of the attempts to abolish the slave trade (Du Bois, 1968).

His next publication was 'The Negroes of Farmville, Virginia: A Social Study,' a U.S. Department of Labor Bulletin, which was published in 1898. 'The Negro in the Black Belt' was published the next year.

These two studies began to establish Du Bois as a first-rate sociological researcher. In 1899 he published *The Philadelphia Negro: A Special Study*. The research was rigorous and reflected the influence of Schmoller and Hart. He began by analyzing the history of the Negroes in Philadelphia and presented data on character, social institutions, and statistics on health, family relations, crime, education, vocational status and literacy. This study was the first sociological text on an Afro-American community published in the United States. Almost fifty years later, Nobel Laureate Gunnar Myrdal described the study as '...one which best meets our requirements' (Marable, 1986). Some of the problems noted in this study still plaque many black communities today. It appears that despite all of Du Bois' efforts and admonitions, the situation has actually exacerbated; there is still racial discrimination and lack of economic justice. Most cities are still, as Du Bois stated, a 'social environment of excuse, listless despair, careless indulgence and lack of inspiration to work.' Due to lack of opportunity for thousands of young black adults, they were unable to develop fully. In this study, Du Bois began to develop what would later become the concept of the Talented Tenth. He observed that the ghetto was a means of ensuring black subordination economically. He stated that Negroes were 'a people receiving a little lower wages than usual for less desirable work, and compelled in order to do that work to live in a less pleasant quarters than most people, and pay for them somewhat higher rents...' He went on to say that the black elite was to accumulate the capital and organize programs to employ black workers. 'The better classes of Negroes should recognize their duty toward the masses. They should not forget that the spirit of the twentieth century is to be the turning of the high toward the lowly, the bending of humanity to all that is human, the recognition that in the slums of modern society lie the answers to most of our puzzling problems of life' (Marable, 1986). There was, however, no clear strategy in this work as to how blacks would advance.

In 1903 Du Bois published the classic *The Souls of Black Folk: Essays and Sketches*. This book received wide and critical acclaim. It included fourteen essays in the areas of political history, sociology and cultural criticism. In the book he calls for democratic rights for all Negroes, and includes a chapter criticizing the Tuskegee Machine. According to James Weldon Johnson, the book had 'a greater effect upon and within the black race in America than any other single book published in this country since *Uncle Tom's Cabin*' (Marable, 1986).

In 1909 Du Bois published the biography *John Brown*. In this book he presented a fresh view of the abolitionist. It was a study in morality and ethics of American society during slavery. In 1915 Du Bois wrote *The Negro*. In this work he traced the history of African peoples and linked that to slavery and the black experience in the New World. He became one of the first to argue that slavery did not destroy all aspects of African culture in the New World. He saw slavery as being for economic exploitation, and called for unity among the workers of the world.

In 1921 he published *Darkwater: Voices from Within the Veil*. In this work he commented that the communist model of social change was inapplicable to the Negro situation in America. Armed revolution, while possible in Africa and Asia, was unthinkable in the United States. Socialism, he stated, had to be 'evolutionary,' not revolutionary. In 1924 he published *The Gift of Black Folk: Negroes in the Making of America*. He described the many 'gifts' black folk have, and yet they were excluded from adequately participating in this democracy. He praised the Catholic Church for its teaching in the South. He advocated 'liberation theology,' a faith that embraces the poor and oppressed.

Du Bois made a major contribution to the Harlem Renaissance with the novel *Dark Princess* in 1928. This book is a love story, with the theme of colored people throughout the world overthrowing colonialism and imperialism. *In Black Reconstruction: An Essay Toward a History of the Part Which Black Folk Played in the Attempt to Reconstruct Democracy in America, 1860-1880*, published in 1935, he related the experience of slavery to democracy and included a critique of racism in American history. He dispelled notions about the reconstruction era, providing information indicating that Reconstruction had failed because it had attempted to further suppress black as well as white labor.

This was followed by *Black Folk Then and Now: An Essay in the History and Sociology of the Negro Race*, published in 1939. In this book he expressed a Marxian perspective in analyzing Negro history. He placed the movements for black equality within a social context of the struggle between capitalists and the proletariat. Du Bois advocated racial segregation for economic strength and the development of all-black economic and social organizations.

In 1940 came *Dusk of Dawn: An Essay Toward An Autobiography of a Race Concept.* In this book Du Bois advocated a Negro 'segregated economy.' Negroes, he stated, could not 'follow the class structure of America…we cannot permit ourselves simply to be victims of exploitation and social exclusion.' He actually criticized his own concept of the Talented Tenth, indicating that it had been rendered irrelevant by the 'whole economic trend of the world.' He recognized that the middle class Negro had not lived up to expectations. Indeed, the idea of the Talented Tenth may have been too idealistic.

Color and Democracy: Colonies and Peace, which was essentially an attack on imperialism and colonialism, was published in 1945. The concept of Pan-Africanism reverberated loudly and clearly throughout the book. In 1947 came *The World and Africa: An Enquiry into the Part Which Africa has Played in the World History*. This built upon his previous research and included information from George Padmore and other Pan-Africans. It was a call for African self-determination. As Paul Robeson observed, '*World and Africa* was one of the first important books on modern postwar Africa and helped to point out and focus attention on the continuing exploitation of Africa by the free world' (Marable, 1986). Kwame Nkrumah and others would utilize it as the building block for some of their theories. In 1952 Du Bois published *In Battle for Peace: The Story of My 83rd Birthday* (Du Bois, 1985).

In 1957 he began his *Black Flame* trilogy about the fictional life of Manuel Marsart, a black intellectual who becomes president of a small black college in Georgia. He utilizes this trilogy and its characters to present his own changing views over 80 years of black history. Du Bois wrote numerous articles, novels and poems, some of which were published. He also wrote many essays for Russian, Belgian, German, French and Chinese audiences. He delivered numerous addresses, wrote pamphlets, weekly columns for newspapers, and introductions and forewords for dozens of volumes, and contributed chapters for books, encyclopedias, and dictionaries. Additionally, he wrote pageants and testified numerous times before governmental bodies (Du Bois, 1968).

Economic Ideas

This section is the crux and focus of this study. Du Bois' extensive writings cover the gamut from philosophy and history to economics and politics.

The influence of the German Historical School's tenets is evident in Du Bois' writings. Du Bois, as a sociologist, historian and economist living in a time of oppression and racial injustice, was of the opinion that the basic problem of race prejudice was an economic one – the lack of economic justice, especially for people of African descent.

Du Bois utilized the evolutionary approach of the German School by considering the historical basis of most of his subjects. He wrote numerous books with a historical perspective. Du Bois' methods were inductive/historical. He concentrated on empirical research, as in the case of *The Philadelphia Negro*. Additionally, his advocacy of conservative reform served as the basis of most of his work. The emphasis was constantly on the proper production and distribution of wealth to satisfy the demands of justice and morality. The nation was to be concerned with the conditions of the 'common man,' who in Du Bois' view was represented by the downtrodden masses of the black Diaspora. All of Du Bois' work centered around the African/Negro plight. Indeed, as a consequence of some of his radical views and continued advocacy for the black races, Du Bois was shunned by white Americans.

On Labor Unions, Economic Exploitation, and Cooperation

Du Bois was in favor of labor unions and of blacks and whites uniting to fight for a common cause, which was the release from class oppression. He was in favor of black and white unity within the labor movement. He issued statements against the exploitation of African nature labor by the imperialists. He realized that racism still existed within the labor unions. As a consequence, Du Bois proposed that whenever possible blacks should initiate their own unions. A. Phillip Randolph's Brotherhood of Sleeping Car Porters, the first successful black union, had been suggested by Du Bois in 1914. Du Bois declared, '...as long as black laborers are slaves, white laborers cannot be free' (Marable, 1986). He called for unity among the working classes. The entire working class (black and white) 'must make one assault upon poverty and race hate.' To begin this process, however, blacks had to form their own separate organizations. As blacks began to cooperate more, there would be greater unity between workers of both races.

Du Bois viewed socialism as a humanistic enterprise based on 'high, ethical ideas.' In *Darkwater*, Du Bois noted, 'All humanity must share in the future industrial democracy of the world. Present Big Business, that Science of Human Wants, must be perfected by eliminating the price paid for Waste, which is Interest, and for Chance which is Profit, and making all income a personal wage for service rendered by the recipient' (Marable, 1986).

Du Bois was also a pacifist who abhorred war. Racism, he declared, was an essential ideological tool to divide workers and maintain domination of capital. World War I, he noted, was the 'result of jealousies engendered by the recent rise of armed national associations of labor and capital, whose aim is the exploitation of the wealth of the world.' Lenin made a similar observation.

For many years during his early career, Du Bois was against revolutionary Marxism. He observed in 1921 (perhaps erroneously) that the theory of class struggle did not apply to black America because that group was not yet divided into capitalists and laborers. Du Bois believed the Negro College should train the best minds without resorting to racism of its own. Segregation was only necessary because blacks were not allowed to compete fairly or equally in an integrated world. Contrary to what is widely known about Du Bois, he was not a segregationist. He stated that 'segregation was evil and should be systematically fought.' However, to combat Jim Crow laws, blacks would do better through collective and cooperative organizations (Marable, 1986).

During the Depression years, Du Bois urged the NAACP to develop a meaningful economic program to assist Negroes. He believed in the formation of economic cooperatives and 'socialization of wealth' among Negroes. He was in favor of preserving government and private agencies in response to the economic crisis by providing some form of relief to those in need (Du Bois, 1968).

Although he never read Marx or Engels during his formative years, Du Bois taught a course, "Karl Marx and the Negro," at Atlanta University in the summer of 1933. In his book *Black Reconstruction* (1935), the influence of Marx is apparent. He critiques American democracy, stating that if all labor (black and white) were freed and given equal rights, it would be difficult for the powers that be to retain control. He described the reconstruction experience in every state in detail. Racism was a means of protecting the prerogatives of capital. He noted that there were class divisions within the Negro community and the 'petty bourgeois' had no distinct plan to uplift the masses, but only to enrich themselves. The real failure of reconstruction, according to Du Bois, was that it intentionally suppressed black as well as white labor. In essence, reconstruction was designed and orchestrated in such a way that it did not attempt to ensure the upliftment of the working class, either black and white (Du Bois, 1935).

In 'A Negro Within the Nation,' an article written in 1935, Du Bois created quite a bit of controversy when he called for Negroes to develop their own program for economic development. He asserted, 'With the use of their political power, their power as consumers...Negroes can develop in the United States an economic nation within a nation, able to work through inner cooperation, to found its own institutions, to educate its genius, and at the same time, without mob violence or extremes of race hatred.' Du Bois was not advocating segregation, just cooperative economics for greater economic power (Marable, 1986).

Du Bois was cognizant of the fact that the Negro laboring classes lacked the wherewithal to lead a program of radical economic reform:

> ...therefore, we must raise a Talented Tenth among us who would become the intelligent leaders and directors of our masses. We must guard against the difficulty that such a Talented Tenth may easily think of itself as the object of its *own efforts*, and think of the masses of Negroes as existing for the aggrandizement of the few...The [elite] must look upon themselves as the servants to do the work for the great mass of the uneducated and inexperienced.

It was the responsibility of the Negro middle class to lead black workers to a moderate socialist program.

In Du Bois' view, accumulating small capital by thrift and then going into business was unrealistic. Blacks had to move strategically toward socialism within the Jim Crow laws. In criticizing the New Deal, Du Bois indicated that it would do very little for blacks or workers of other races. To the Talented Tenth he admonished, 'if the leading Negro classes cannot assume and bear the uplift of their own proletariat, they are doomed for time and eternity' (Marable, 1968).

Du Bois' theories were deemed radical in his day. Contrary to Marx, Du Bois called for cooperation rather than revolution. The concept of cooperation is not an anathema to any group; it is practiced by Asian Americans, Jewish-Americans, and others. Why not by African-Americans? His call was for unity among the oppressed for greater power, which would then lead to an equitable distribution of wealth within a social system. Du

Bois believed this was possible as long as the power was not abused by the Talented Tenth, thereby distancing themselves further from the masses.

On Democracy, Colonialism, Pan-Africanism and Socialism

Although a pacifist, Du Bois argued in favor of the Second World War, noting that the war could be waged to expand democratic rights for oppressed nations and thirty-three peoples. Despite his views about socialism, he did not believe that the communism in Russia was appropriate for a minority group such as the blacks in America. He attempted to separate the political concept of democracy from the political economy of capitalism. According to Du Bois, the democracy being defended did not exist. Once fascism was destroyed, a new definition of democracy would be created worldwide. In 1943 Du Bois called for an alternative to the segregationist-controlled United States Congress. This alternative would be based on popular participation and open discussion. In Du Bois' view, real democracy involved state planning for production, the eradication of unemployment and poverty, women's inequality, anti-Semitism, and anti-racist violence. In a 1942 unpublished paper, Du Bois states, 'Democracy is not, as so many of us are prone to think, simply the right of electing our rulers. It is not simply, as others think, the right of working people to have a choice in the conduct of industry. It is much more than this, it is a vaster and more inclusive ideal; it is the right to accumulate and use a great reservoir of human thought and experience, out of which a people may choose…the wisest and best policies of government and conduct.' For Du Bois, democracy was an all-inclusive concept, which meant the abolition of all forms of domination, including European colonialism and the granting of full self-determination for all oppressed peoples. At a commencement address at Talladega College in 1944, Du Bois stated, almost in a Marxist vein, 'The great majority of men, the poverty-stricken and diseased are the real workers of the world….Their future path is clear. It is to accumulate such knowledge and balance of judgment that they can reform the world, so that the workers of the world receive just share of the wealth which they make and that all human beings who are capable of work shall work' (Du Bois, 1986).

Du Bois was so concerned about exploitation of the masses that in 1937 he defined Pan-Africanism as 'a movement to begin a leadership of the exploited among the most exploited, with the idea of its ultimate expansion to the colored laboring class and workers of all colors throughout the world.'

Du Bois related the situation of American Negroes to that of the colonial peoples in Africa, stating that they were similar in economic and political status.   He abhorred imperialism and observed that the future of the American Negro hinged on that of other colonial peoples in the world.   In order for peace to reign, Du Bois observed that if the oppressed were to be 'released from poverty, ignorance, and disease,' worldwide democracy must apply to the masses, and most struggles would end. After his 1936 trip to the Soviet Union, Du Bois observed, 'Russia says that the bread for the million masses is more important than diamond rings for the hundreds....The only hope of human unity lies in the common cause, the common interest of the working classes, in Europe, Africa, and Asia' (Du Bois, 1986).

As director of research for the NAACP, Du Bois felt it was incumbent on the group to structure a progressive economic agenda designed to eliminate poverty and to 'curb monopoly and the role of wealth, spread education and practice democracy.'   Du Bois saw socialism as the solution to the Negro's problems. He declared in 1947, 'Socialism is an attack on poverty. We can by our knowledge, by use of our democratic power, prevent the concentration of political and economic power in the hands of the monopolists who rule colonies.' He went on to add, 'Every leading land on earth is moving toward socialism, so as to restrict the power of wealth, introduce democratic methods in industry, and stop the persistence of poverty in its children, ignorance, disease, and crime' (Marable, 1986).

Du Bois viewed President Roosevelt's New Deal as some movement of the United States toward socialism – in such vast undertakings as the Tennessee Valley Authority, in providing jobs for the unemployed during the Depression, and in seeking to aid works of art and literature. He saw the Soviet model as one that could eliminate poverty and unemployment – the most hopeful state in the world today. He also observed that the Soviets had become the greatest proponent of colonial independence (Marable, 1986).

Talented Tenth

According to Du Bois, the Talented Tenth theory was a strategy that would lead to democracy for all black Americans. It is those of the race best prepared and qualified by means of education and economic status who should serve as the beacons. It was to spur those in the middle class to regard the plight of the less fortunate as their own. This is reminiscent not only of the German Historical influence (conservative reform), but also the influence of Josiah Royce, Du Bois' Harvard professor.

These Talented Tenth were to take up the fight to uplift the masses for collective economic improvement.   This concept is summed up in the following statement: '...The [elite] must look upon themselves as the servants to do the work for the great mass of the uneducated and inexperienced.' This theory was used by Booker T. Washington and others as evidence of Du Bois' isolation from the masses (Marable, 1986). Du Bois did not intend for blacks to completely neglect vocational training; he was determined that blacks not be satisfied with vocational training and the accumulation of wealth. This was in stark contrast to the accommodationism of the Tuskegee machine. It is now widely accepted that the methods of both Du Bois and Washington are necessary for progress in the black community.

Revising his Talented Tenth thesis, Du Bois addressed the issue of the few committing themselves and sacrificing their wealth in such a way as to uplift the entire group. As the years wore on he became concerned, as he should have been, that an 'exploiting class could emerge within the black community.' He asserted in his Talented Tenth series that it was possible the Talented Tenth would fail to supply the leadership for the working classes. Indeed, a majority had failed to do so. He believed that the real leadership would come from 'intelligent and better paid workers.' There were class divisions within the black community itself.

He stated in no uncertain terms that racism was born out of the capitalist economy. 'Behind the dilemma of racism lies a greater problem which both obscures and implements it: and that is the fact that so many civilized persons are willing to live in comfort even if the price of this is poverty, and disease of the majority of their fellow man.'

After joining the Communist party in 1961, Du Bois made the following statement (Marable, 1986):

> Capitalism cannot reform itself, it is doomed to self-destruction. No universal selfishness can bring social good to all. Communism – the effort to give all men what they need and to ask of each the best they can contribute – this is the only way of human life. It is a difficult and hard end to reach, it has and will make mistakes, but today it marches triumphantly on in education and science, in home and food, with increased freedom of thought and deliverance from dogma. In the end communism will triumph. I want to help bring that day. The path of the American Communist Party is clear: It will provide the United States with a real Third party and thus restore democracy to this land.

Critical Analysis of Du Bois' Views

Much like any of the economists we study in history of economic thought, their times shaped their ideas and writings. Although a scholar of great intellect, Du Bois was not given his due recognition by society for several reasons. First, he was a radical and controversial individual whose views in many instances were anathema to white society. Second, he never held a substantial position at a majority institution. Third, his views conflicted with the most powerful blacks of his day, Booker T. Washington and Marcus Garvey. Fourth, his writings dealt with a minority group about whom very few were concerned.

It is also easy to overlook Du Bois' contributions as an economist because society had viewed and portrayed him more as a historian and sociologist. Additionally, Du Bois never wrote a strictly economic text. Furthermore, very few are truly familiar with his work in Berlin under the German Historical School's Gustav Schmoller.

Here we analyze critically three of Du Bois' economic ideas: (1) the concept of the Talented Tenth, (2) his views of the labor class and exploitation, and (3) his views on Pan-Africanism, colonialism and imperialism.

The Talented Tenth

It is for this concept that Du Bois is most recognized. This concept simply states that the educated few can uplift the many. Du Bois himself noted in 1940 that this concept made 'naïve' assumptions. In Du Bois' first study of the Negro population of Philadelphia in 1903, he noted the poverty, crime and hopelessness that pervaded the Negro ghettos. Since then, blacks have come a long way, but the situation for the masses has not improved. The Talented Tenth have failed to hold up their end of the bargain. There are now more pronounced class divisions within the black community.

Much like Marx, other socialists, Schmoller and other members of the German Historical School believed that assuming man would not behave in a self-interested manner is erroneous. The classical tenet of self-interested behavior is without a doubt veracious. We are all driven by the self-interest motive. Even a member of the Talented Tenth who dedicates himself to uplifting the masses (as Du Bois did) does so for purely selfish reasons – the satisfaction and utility gained from seeing others uplifted. Unfortunately, as Du Bois feared, as the Talented Tenth developed they felt no allegiance to the masses and began to integrate into white society. More often than not, an African-American who attains a certain level of success moves to the suburbs to distance himself/herself from the downtrodden masses. This is perhaps a natural law of self-preservation. Hence, class conflicts began to arise within the black community itself as the black bourgeoisie capitalists sought to further distance themselves from the 'undesirable' Negroes.

Exploitation of the Working Class

Du Bois saw the Negro working class as the most exploited group of workers in the world. He viewed Negro labor along with that of the white laboring class as the most disadvantaged group in the economy. His view was socialist, if not Marxist. He called for workers all around the world to unite to fight for their rights. This unity, according to Du Bois, first had to begin with the Negro workers forming cooperatives, guided by the Talented Tenth since the laborers themselves did not have the wherewithal to unite. He favored unions and suggested the formation of unions along racial lines, since many blacks were excluded from white unions. Unlike Marx, his call for an uprising was not by armed conflict, but by the workers gaining more education to better themselves. In his view, these workers would then resort to a socialist system and seek the ideals of the entire society.

This socialist view, while indeed factual in terms of labor exploitation, has the same shortcomings as all socialist points of view. It fails to recognize, again, that individuals are driven by their own self-interest and that there is a natural tendency to move away from socialism. Class conflicts would begin to increase even as the workers removed the yoke of exploitation. What would happen as these workers moved up? The problems probably would persist.

Pan-Africanism, Imperialism and Colonialism

Du Bois was the father of Pan-Africanism. He was one of the first to cry out against the injustices of the colonial powers who exploited Africa for their own gain. Africa, he said, must be for the Africans. While in Germany, although Du Bois did not experience racism, he heard a lecture by the German, Von Treitschke, who stated that mulattoes were inferior. Friedrich List, a member of the older German Historical School, had written and believed strongly that manufacturing could only develop in the temperate zone. The tropical areas were more suited for agriculture and its inhabitants could not develop the intelligence to manufacture (Brue, 1994).

Pan-Africanism called for the economic cooperation of all the exploited masses in the African Diaspora. Africans were to unite in spirit with African-Americans to lift the yoke of oppression. He called for economic cooperation of all colored peoples around the world. With Du Bois' help and the Pan-African conferences, there was a push for African self-sufficiency and independence. Today, with the help of Du Bois, Nkrumah, Padmore and others, most of Africa is free. Du Bois was the father of African independence. The major problem with all calls for unity is that it is doubtful whether the oppressed really wish to unite. Perhaps this is because after years of oppression the oppressed may wish to take charge and become oppressors themselves. This is what has occurred over and over again since the demise of colonialism. In Africa, the Africans themselves are oppressing and suppressing each other. There is mass corruption, civil war, and in most instances these nations are worse off than they were 30 or 40 years ago.

Conclusion

'A prophet is not accepted in his own country.' This is a paraphrase of a statement made by Jesus Christ of Nazareth. Du Bois, despite his numerous achievements, did not receive the recognition he so richly deserved until after his death. Indeed, he was compelled to move to Ghana, where he died.

Born in Massachusetts, Du Bois felt he had something to say to the world and set about doing so. After moving to the South to attend college, Du Bois became more familiar with the economic conditions of blacks. Du Bois possessed a personality that sometimes seemed aloof. He was a difficult person to get close to, yet he was compassionate and caring and was immensely concerned about the plight of not only the blacks in the Diaspora, but also of the oppressed workers of the world. Du Bois was at various points in time a socialist and communist, but always a radical. Du Bois was a pioneer in the truest sense of the word. A controversial figure, he appeared to waiver on various issues, however, his views were simply reflective of the times and circumstances. Although during his lifetime he received numerous honors, he never held a position at a major white institution and never received an honorary degree from any of them.

Internationally, he received greater recognition. Du Bois' numerous honors include the following: fellow and life member of the American Association for the Advancement of Sciences, member of the National Institute of Arts and Letters, Knight Commander of the Liberian Order of African Redemption, and recipient of the International and Lenin Peace Prizes (Du Bois, 1984). Paradoxically, today, a major white institution, the University of Massachusetts in Amherst, has a library named after Du Bois. In 1973 his widow, Shirley Graham, donated some of his papers to the library, which was then dedicated in his name. Additionally, there are lectures in his name, numerous exhibits and a research center, which is the nation's oldest research center dedicated to the study of history, culture and social sciences.

Du Bois' concept of the Talented Tenth would prove efficacious if the common man were altruistic. Unfortunately, most people are not. Most individuals seem to lack that selflessness necessary to transcend self in order to concentrate on developing society. Many of his concepts are still popular in certain circles. Upon his death, the journal he had founded, *Crisis*, proclaimed him 'the prime inspirer, philosopher, and father of the Negro protest movement' (Bigelow, 1993). In this sense he was the forerunner of Martin Luther King, Jr., Kwame Nkrumah, Malcolm X and others. Based on his writings and economic pronouncements, he was the first black economist of the modern era.

4 Sir W. Arthur Lewis – Development Economist and Nobel Laureate (1915-1990)

Sir W. Arthur Lewis is the first modern economist considered in this study. He is a true economic theorist and pioneer in the field of economic development.

We proceed by looking at his biographical background and career. We then analyze his theories and contributions to determine their validity and long-lasting value. Finally, we consider the various criticisms that have been leveled against his theories in order to determine their validity.

Lewis is the only black to ever win the Nobel Prize in economics. He was also the first black Nobel Laureate in an area other than peace. He shared this prize in 1979 with Theodore Schultz. Lewis was born in St. Lucia, West Indies on January 23, 1915. He was British educated, earning a degree from the London School of Economics. He earned graduate degrees from the University of Manchester and the University of London. He taught at the London School of Economics for ten years. In 1948 he began teaching at the University of Manchester, where he remained for ten years. He later became principal and vice-chancellor of the University of the West Indies (Blaug, 1985).

The positions held by Lewis (knighted in Britain in 1963) have been exemplary. They include the following: instructor, London School of Economics; professor of economics, University of Manchester; member of the United National Group of Experts on Underdeveloped Countries; consultant to the Gold Coast and Western Nigeria; economic advisor to the Prime Minister of Ghana; principal, University College of the West Indies; vice-chancellor, University of the West Indies (1962); professor of economics, Princeton University; president, Caribbean Development Bank; chancellor, University of Ghana (honorary 1966-73); and president, American Economic Association (1982) (Blaug, 1985). Lewis died in 1991.

Biographical Background (Lewis, 1980)

Lewis was born in St. Lucia, a small island in the Lesser Antilles in the Caribbean Sea. The island remained under British rule until independence in 1979. His parents, who were both schoolteachers, had emigrated there from Antigua approximately twelve years before.

He was a precocious youth whose progress through the public schools was accelerated. When he was seven he had to stay home for several months because of an ailment, whereupon his father elected to teach him so that he would not fall behind. He learned in three months as much as the school taught in two years; upon returning to school he was promoted from grade 4 to grade 6. The rest of his school life and early working life, up to age 18, was spent with fellow students or workers two or three years his elder.

His father died when he was seven, leaving a widow and five sons ranging in age from five to seventeen. His mother was the most highly disciplined and hardest working person he had ever known, and this, combined with her love and gentleness, enabled her to make a success of each of her children.

He left school at age 14, having completed the curriculum, and went to work as a clerk in the civil service. His next step would be to sit for the examination for a St. Lucia government scholarship to a British university, but he was too young for this until 1932. In his position as clerk he learned to type, file and be orderly.

In 1932 he took the examination and won the scholarship. At this point he was confused about what to do with his life. The British government imposed a color ban in its colonies, so young blacks studied only law or medicine, professions they could make a living from without government support. Lewis did not want to be a lawyer or a doctor; he wanted to be an engineer, but this seemed pointless since neither the government nor the white firms would employ a black engineer. Eventually he decided to study business administration, planning to return to St. Lucia for a job in the municipal service or in the private trade. He would simultaneously study law to fall back on if nothing administrative turned up. He attended the London School of Economics to pursue a bachelor's degree in commerce, which offered accounting, business management, commercial law, and a little economics and statistics.

He, like many youths today, had no idea in 1933 what economics was, but he did well in the subject from the start. He graduated in 1937 with first class honors, and earned a scholarship to pursue a Ph.D. in industrial economics.

In 1938 he was given a one-year teaching appointment, which was sensational for British universities. This was converted into the usual four-year contract for an assistant lecturer in 1939. Lewis states, 'My foot was now on the ladder, and the rest was up to me. My luck held, and I rose rapidly. In 1948, at 33, I was made a full professor at the University of Manchester.'

Until he went to Manchester his field of study was industrial economics, and he published a series of articles on the subject, which culminated in a book in 1949. The leading practitioner of this art at the London School of Economics was Professor Sir Arnold Plant, a *laissez-faire* liberal.

Lewis' research has been in three areas: industrial economics, the history of the world economy since 1870, and development economics (which he did not begin systematically until about 1950).

He was influenced to expand his horizons by Frederick Hayek, then acting chairman of the Department of Economics at the London School of Economics, who encouraged him to teach a course in the history of world economy. He continued to lecture on this subject for many years, and published a book on it in 1949. Among the questions that the book did not answer was whether or not the Great Depression of 1929 was part of a cycle stretching back into the nineteenth century. Data for the years prior to 1914 were sparse and unreliable, and he could not proceed faster than additions to the data and revisions would permit. He spent a lot of time with the data and, between 1952 and 1957, published a stream of articles on world production, prices and trade from 1870 to 1914. However, he could never finish the book. In 1957, just as he was ready to complete it, he went into administration for six years. He returned to the book in 1963 in his new professorship at Princeton University, and found that the four or five researchers in 1952 had now multiplied into a crowd of writers on the subject. He returned to improvement of the data and was ready to write his book when he went to Barbados for four years to set up the Caribbean Development Bank. Returning to Princeton in 1974, he finally published in 1978 his account of growth and fluctuations in the world economy between 1870 and 1914.

Lewis' interest in development economics arose when he spent time in the Colonial Office Library reading reports from the colonial territories on agricultural problems, mining, currency questions and other issues. By comparing different territories, he learned about the efficacy of different policies. He did some lecturing on this subject to colonial students at the London School of Economics in the 1940s, but it was the multitude of Asian and African students at Manchester that set him lecturing on development economics from about 1950.

The other half of his interest was in the fundamental forces determining the rate of economic growth. From that interest came the classic publication in 1950, *Economic Development with Unlimited Supplies of Labour*, in which he developed the theory for which he later won the Nobel Prize.

He was appointed reader in colonial economics while a lecturer at the London School of Economics, which enabled him to focus on research affecting the British colonies. This further piqued his interest in development economics. He later moved to Manchester University where he occupied the Stanley Jevons chair of political economy from 1948 to 1958. During this period he wrote a series of seminal works, which included his book *The Theory of Economic Growth*, written in 1955, and his groundbreaking article 'Economic Development with Unlimited Supplies of Labour.'

In spite of his successes at Manchester, Lewis felt a calling to return home to the West Indies and make a contribution. In 1959 he accepted a position as principal at the University College of the West Indies. He helped secure autonomy for the institution from the University of London. In 1962 he was appointed vice-chancellor (president) of the University of the West Indies.

In 1968 he journeyed to the United States and was appointed professor of public and international affairs at Princeton and, later, as James Madison professor of political economy at the same institution. In 1970 he took a position as the first president of the Caribbean Development Bank. He almost simultaneously served as chancellor of the University of Guyana from 1966 to 1973. He returned to Princeton in 1973.

Concerned about poverty eradication and the development problem in the developing world, Lewis worked with several developing countries. He served as a consultant to the Caribbean Commission, United National Economic Commission for Asia and the Far East, Gold Coast Government, West Nigerian Government, and was advisor to the prime minister of Ghana (Kwame Nkrumah) from 1957 to 1958 and to the prime minister of the West Indies Federation. He also served as a member of the United Nations Group of Exports on Underdeveloped Countries and deputy managing director of the United Nations Special Fund. Lewis drafted the first development plan for Trinidad and Tobago and co-authored the Pearson Commission Report.

Lewis was knighted in 1963, and received numerous honorary degrees. He also served as president of the American Economic Association. He continued as a member of the Princeton faculty until his death in 1991.

Theories and Major Contributions

In his book *Theorists of Economic Growth from David Hume to the Present*, W. W. Rostow, himself an eminent growth theorist, lists Lewis as one of nine economic growth pioneers. As Rostow states, 'Lewis is also unique among the development economists...his *Economic Growth* is the only study that touches on all the key growth variables' (Rostow, 1990). He has written extensively on economic development and growth. His career emphasis was on economic growth as it is impacted by unlimited supplies of labor and how agriculture impacts economic growth.

Lewis' first publication was 'An Economic Plan for Jamaica.' This was followed by *Economic Survey; Overhead Costs: The Principles of Economic Planning*; *The Theory of Economic Growth*; *Development Planning: The Essentials of Economic Planning; Tropical Development 1880-1913; The Evolution of International Economic Order;* and *Growth and Fluctuations*, to name a few (Blaug, 1985).

The Economic Development Model

Lewis' scholarship and contributions to economics are numerous.   He realized that economic development analysis is multi-disciplinary and pragmatic. He practiced what he preached. He saw development plans as a means of eradicating poverty in the developing world.

Lewis' two-sector or dual economic development model is his claim to fame and the reason he was awarded the Nobel Prize in 1979.

Drawing on classical theory and the historical experiences of the western industrialized nations, Lewis developed a two-sector model of economic development, dividing the economy into a rural subsistence sector and a modern urban industrial sector. He points out that the rural sector has an abundance or surplus of labor that could easily be transferred to the urban sector with no loss in agricultural output. With a more profitable urban sector, the rural poor would naturally be attracted to the urban sector. Since wages in the rural area are lower than in the urban area, employers can hire as many rural workers as they wish, earn profits, reinvest a portion, and increase wages. As the process continues, output expands and economic growth follows (Brue, 1994). In his *Theory of Economic Growth*, Lewis touches on all the key growth variables: (1) population and the working force, (2) capital and technology, (3) business cycles, (4) relative prices, (5) stages and limits to growth and (6) non-economic factors.

On Economic Planning

In *The Principles of Economic Planning* (1949), Lewis emphasized planning through the market, as opposed to planning by direction. He warned against the bureaucracy of planning by direction, as it tends to be imprecise, inflexible, too standardized and stifling. He writes:

> On account of its complexity, planning by direction does not increase, but on the contrary diminishes democratic control. A plan cannot be made by the people or by parliament or by the cabinet; it has to be made by officials, because it consists of thousands of details fitted together. Its results are embodied in thousands of administrative orders and decisions, of which parliament and ministers can have only the briefest knowledge, and which provide innumerable opportunities for corrupting the public service. The more we direct from the center the less the control that is possible. When the government is doing only a few things, we can keep an eye on it, but when it is doing everything it cannot even keep an eye on itself.

Lewis knew well how to superimpose economics on politics. He utilized economic tools to analyze politics. In *Politics in West Africa* (1965), Lewis stated that politicians were naturally concerned with personal gain:

> Politicians like to be thought of as heroes, but in fact they are just like other men, and to earn their respect and gratitude for great achievement; at the same time we need money, power and prestige to fulfill our personalities. Economic philosophers insist that it is absurd to devise an economic system on the assumption that men are motivated mainly by a desire to serve; on the contrary, the function of a good economic system is to transmute into social benefit the drive for personal gain which keeps the system going. This is achieved (or sought) by a system of controls which tries to ensure that money can be made only by serving the public: only by offering the market what it wants. Businessmen seek constantly to escape these controls; strengthening the market to prevent manipulation is one of the continuing tasks of economic democracy. The same applies to political systems. Politicians, like businessmen, are motivated by the desire for money, power and prestige as well as the desire to serve. A good political system assumes that politicians are ordinary men and seeks through its control to ensure that politicians can fulfill their personal ambitions only by serving the public. A political system whose functioning depended on the altruism of politicians would be just as much an absurdity as an economic system depending upon the altruism of businessmen. The essence of political democracy is that the politicians are subordinate to the public, in whom are vested the fundamental rights of free criticism, opposition and dismissal. A political system in which the public surrenders these rights to a political party

must have the same evil results as an economic system in which the market is subordinated to a build of businessmen.

On International Trade

In addition to the basic concept of the dual economy, there were the seeds of another theory at the end of Lewis' paper on 'surplus labor.' Lewis developed a Ricardian Model comparing the rich temperate zone countries and poor tropical countries in terms of trade, favoring the richer nation due to immigration quality and compensation for labor. He states (Lewis, 1994):

> The factorial terms available to the tropics, on the other hand, offered the opportunity to stay poor at any rate until such time as the labour reservoirs of India and China might be exhausted. A farmer of Nigeria might tend his peanuts with as much diligence and skill as a farmer in Australia tended his sheep, but the return would be very different. The just price, to use the medieval term, would have rewarded equal competence with equal earnings. But the market price gave the Nigerian for his peanuts a 700 lbs. of grain per acre level of living, and the Australian for his wool a 1600 lbs. per acre level of living, not because of differences in competence, nor because of marginal utilities or productivities in peanuts or wool, but because these were the respective amounts of food which their cousins could produce on the family farms. This is the fundamental sense in which the leaders of the less developed world denounce the current international economic order as unjust, namely that the factorial terms of trade are based on the market forces of opportunity cost, and not on the just principle of equal pay for equal work. And of course nobody understood this mechanism better than the working classes in the temperate settlements themselves, and in the U.S.A. They were always adamant against Indian or Chinese immigration into their countries because they realized that, if unchecked, it must drive wages down close to Indian and Chinese levels.

He also realized that in order for the developing nations to progress, they would have to do so primarily on their own with assistance from the developed nations.

Validity and Analysis of Contributions

Born in St. Lucia in the West Indies, Lewis was unlike many of the other growth theorists in that he actually hailed from the developing world. His *Economic Growth* was the first study to touch on all the key growth variables (Rostow, 1990). His work was unique and differed from theorists of the time because it focused on the growth process in developing countries (distinct from the theories of Harrod, Domar and Solow, which focused on advanced capitalist nations).

In many instances, Lewis' two-sector model is valid. Surplus labor transferred from the rural sector to the urban sector will assist in economic growth. This process is similar to that experienced by the United States and other industrialized nations, especially the 'Little Tigers' of Southeast Asia (Taiwan, Korea, etc.).

It is easy, however, to find fault with his theory since the modern Third World nations do not appear to be following this pattern of development. Some individuals have criticized the views of Lewis. As one who lived in the developing world, he sought only to provide solutions. His views are very positive. As Lewis states (Rostow, 1990):

Taken as a group, governments of less developed countries (LDCs) have, in fact, passed reasonable tests. There are four times as many children in school as there were in 1950. The infant mortality rate has fallen by three-quarters. The multiplication of hospital beds, village water pipes, all-season village roads, and other mass services is faster than at any period in the history of the countries now developed. Much of the disillusionment with the results of the past three decades originates with people who do not understand the importance of the social wage, who have no idea what the conditions of the masses were like in 1950, or who have forgotten the extent to which LDC peoples live in semi-arid lands for which we have yet to make the technological breakthrough.

Michael Todaro, one of Lewis' most prominent critics, noted that despite recent urban migration, these nations are still less developed (Brue, 1994). He notes that the rural-urban migration has created mass unemployment and urban squalor. Urban wage rates have also increased, not remaining constant as Lewis' model assumed. While these criticisms are valid, it is worth noting that his model did not assume unlimited rural-urban migration. This author's contention is that many of these nations may have already reached the point of diminishing returns for labor. The solution, then, would be to reduce the rural-urban migration at the point where surplus labor and, consequently, unemployment and under-employment are created in the urban areas. During the initial stages of a nation's development, Lewis' model proves valid. The model becomes suspect once we get beyond the initial stages.

In the 1950s, 1960s, and 1970s the Third World nations were making progress. The most recent failures are due largely to misplaced priorities as a result of poor management by the leaders of these nations. The classical tenet of self-interested behavior in this case holds; that of harmony of interests proves inadequate.

Lewis has had numerous critics, some of whom have actually made a career out of critiquing his work. Some of the criticism focused on Lewis' theory is that there could be so much surplus labor in the rural or subsistence sector that the marginal product of labor would be zero, thus enabling labor transfer to occur without a decrease in the total product or output. They contended that as labor transfer occurred, the average wages and, thus, income would rise among those remaining. This meant that wages would rise in the model, not remain constant.

Another criticism is that the model ignores the creation of a capitalist class in the urban areas as the surplus labor transfer occurs. Capitalists are not likely to automatically reinvest all of their profits. Other critics pointed to the exploitation of the developing economies by the developed ones, thus rendering Lewis' assumptions invalid, they said. Furthermore, there could be internal exploitation by capitalists who take advantage of the masses who crowd the urban areas.

Lewis responded to his critics by emphasizing that his dual economies were the 'capitalist' and 'subsistence' sectors, not urban and rural or industrial and agriculture. He states that the model actually described what had happened in some nations.

Lewis showed how labor and investment patterns work internationally. He stated the conditions for sufficient investments to occur in a nation. First, wages had to be at a level indicating there was sufficient labor that could be utilized profitably. Second, the work force had to be skilled enough to work profitably. Until this happened, few, if any, investments would flow into that nation. Numerous nations, such as those in Southeast Asia and most recently China, fall in this category. Yet others, such as many of the sub-Saharan African countries, have performed dismally (Houseman and Maung, 1992).

Lewis' theory and observations are valid when considered in the broad context. Many nations, such as the United States and Japan, have followed this pattern of development. There are, however, problems with the theory, as it does not sufficiently account for political instability, technological change, exploitation, and numerous other variables. The problem of economic development is a complex one that involves a multitude of variables. Lewis' model provided the groundwork from which to build. Incorporating his basic model (which is still discussed in economic development texts) with others and taking into account certain key variables is the best course of action. The model, in a historical and systematic sense, cannot be discarded.

As Lewis stated in 1984, 'If conflict and disputes are indices to intellectual activity, our subject (development economics) seems adequately contentious' (Brue, 1994).

5 Kwame Nkrumah – The African Socialist (1909-1972)

We turn our attention to the African continent again. In this chapter we consider the contributions of Kwame Nkrumah, arguably the greatest African leader of the twentieth century.

Like Du Bois, Nkrumah is not typically regarded as an economist; however, based upon his studies, scholarship and contributions, there is no doubt that he was a Marxist or socialist economist. We begin by considering Nkrumah's biographical background, his career, and then his writings and contributions. Finally, we analyze his contributions to determine their long-lasting value and validity.

Biographical Sketch

Kwame Nkrumah was born Francis Nwia Kofie into the Akan tribe in Nkroful located in the Western Province of the Gold Coast (now Ghana) in 1909 (Nkrumah, 1957). His father was a petty artisan who made and sold jewelry. His mother sold produce at the local market and worked in the fields. He was an only child, although he had numerous half-siblings. He had the utmost affection for his mother, and later when he was president said, 'My mother is a tower of strength to me...I have never cared for any woman as much as I have cared for her. We are both alike in one thing – we seem to draw strength from each other. In the same way I feel better for seeing her, she gets better if she is ill and I visit her' (Marais, 1972). Both of Nkrumah's parents were illiterate, however, they impressed upon him the importance of education. He attended a Catholic elementary school where all of the instructors were European.

Nkrumah was baptized a Roman Catholic. After completing eight years of schooling near the top of his class he was employed as a pupil teacher at a local primary school.

In 1927 Nkrumah enrolled at Accra Training in Accra, the Ghanaian capital. During the same year his father died. Nkrumah was then influenced by Dr. Kwegyir Aggrey, a Ghanaian educated in the United States who served as director of Prince of Wales College in Achimota, the first institution of higher education in the Gold Coast. Aggrey believed that the education was too Eurocentric and did not emphasize knowledge relating to that which was African. This awakened a sense of national pride in the young Nkrumah. Soon after developing a relationship with Nkrumah, Aggrey died (Nkrumah, 1965).

In 1928 the Accra Training College was combined with Prince of Wales. The curriculum was decidedly British. Nkrumah observed (Davidson, 1989):

> ...curriculum, discipline and sports were as close imitations as possible of those operating in English public schools. The object was to train up a western oriented political elite committed to the attitudes and ideologies of capitalism and bourgeois society.

Already, he was beginning to realize the unlawfulness of the colonial government.

Nkrumah secured a position as a teacher at a Catholic junior school in Elmina. After one year he became headmaster of the Catholic junior school in Aksima. It was here that he encountered his first political mentor, Samuel R. Wood, then secretary of the National Congress of British West Africa. During this time there was unrest in the Gold Coast. Nnamdi Azikiwe, who would become the first president of Nigeria, served as a journalist in Ghana and wrote articles that influenced Nkrumah.

In 1935 Nkrumah was admitted to Lincoln University in Pennsylvania, Azikiwe's alma mater. During the summers of the Great Depression he sold fish in New York. He eventually secured a position as a dishwasher on a ship, and subsequently became a waiter and messenger. In 1939 he graduated from Lincoln University with a degree in economics and sociology. He took a position as a philosophy assistant at Lincoln. In 1942 he earned a bachelor's degree in theology from Lincoln and a master's degree in education from Pennsylvania University. In 1943 he defended his thesis in philosophy, passed his doctoral exams, and began his dissertation. He worked at a shipbuilding yard while in school, working so hard that he fell ill, thus causing him not to complete his dissertation. While conducting research in Philadelphia he saw the miserable conditions under which black Americans lived. He realized that the conditions of the colonial Africans and the African-Americans were very similar. He became interested in W. E. B. Du Bois and Marcus Garvey, and was convinced that he had to return to Ghana and form a political party to change the status quo (Smertin, 1990).

Nkrumah was instrumental in organizing the African conference in New York to adopt a resolution to push for African independence. Paul Robeson was involved in this effort and influenced Nkrumah.

In 1945 Nkrumah left the United States for England. There he joined George Padmore's Pan-African movement in seeking improved conditions for colonial Africa. He was secretary of the organization's committee for the fifth Pan-African Congress, chaired by Du Bois.

In 1947 Nkrumah returned to Ghana as general secretary of the United Gold Coast Convention (UGCC). Nkrumah's radical views led to his arrest and removal from leadership of the UGCC. In 1949 Nkrumah formed the Convention People's Party (CPP). Due to the CCP's activities, Nkrumah was arrested and sentenced to three years in prison. He was released from prison when the CPP won elections in 1951. In 1952 Nkrumah became prime minister of the Gold Coast. He was Africa's first black prime minister.

Nkrumah served as prime minister of Ghana until 1960, when he assumed the presidency. He supported a militant anti-colonial policy and opposed neocolonialism – indirect Western influence exercised through economic pressure. In 1966 the army seized power while Nkrumah was out of the country. He went to live in Guinea where he served as co-president. He died in Romania of cancer.

During his life Nkrumah held numerous positions, including the following: secretary of the Pan-African Congress; general secretary, West African National Secretariat; general secretary, United Gold Coast Convention (UGCC); chairman, Convention People's Party (CPP); prime minister, Gold Coast; president of Ghana; and co-president of Guinea (honorary).

It is for Nkrumah's economic training and economic theories that he is included in this study. He was an economist, albeit in the Marxist vein.

Contributions to Economic Theory

Nkrumah was a prolific writer in the areas of politics and economics as it pertained to Africa. His economic/political theories may be gleaned from his many writings. His written works include the following: *Toward Colonial Freedom* (1945); *Neo-Colonialism: The Last Stages of Imperialism; I Speak of Freedom; Africa Must Unite; Dark Days in Ghana; Consciencism: Philosophy and Ideology for Decolonization* (1964); *Handbook of Revolutionary Warfare: A Guide to the Armed Phase of the African Revolution; Class Struggle in Africa;* and *The Autobiography of Kwame*

Nkrumah: Black Star (Bigelow, 1993). He was undoubtedly influenced by Marx, Lenin and Mao. It is in the context of these writings that we develop Nkrumah's economic ideas. His political/economic thoughts may be summed up in a concept known as Nkrumahism – an African-specific Marxist/Socialist concept.

As he so appropriately states in *Toward Colonial Freedom* (Smertin, 1990):

> Existence for the colonial peoples under imperialist rule means their economic and political exploitation. The imperialist powers need the materials and cheap native labour of the colonies for their own capitalist industries. Through their system of monopolist control they eliminate native competition, and use the colonies as dumping grounds for their surplus mass-produced goods. In attempting to legitimize their presence they claim to be improving the welfare of the native population. Such claims are merely a camouflage for their real purpose of exploitation to which they are driven by economic necessity. Whether the dependent territory is administered as a colony, protectorate or mandate, it is all part of an imperialist plan to perpetuate its economic exploitation. The colonies gain no advantages whatsoever from being dependent; socially and technologically their progress is hindered; they pay for a nominal protection against aggression by providing troops for the mother country in time of war and their freedom will never be automatically granted but won by their endeavors. Britain may claim that she holds the colonies under trusteeship until they are capable of self-government, but it is not in her interests to relinquish her stranglehold. The African, however, was perfectly capable of governing himself before the advent of the white man and should be allowed to do so again...

In *Neo-colonialism: The Last Stage of Imperialism* (1966), Nkrumah writes (*Crisis*, 1999):

> The Neocolonialism of today represents imperialism in its final and perhaps its most dangerous stage. In the past it was possible to convert a country upon which a neo-colonial regime had been imposed – Egypt in the nineteenth century is an example – into a colonial territory. Today this process is no longer feasible.

> Old-fashioned colonialism is by no means entirely abolished. It still constitutes an African problem, but it is everywhere on the retreat. Once a territory has become nominally independent, it is no longer possible, as it was in the last century, to reverse the process. In place of colonialism as the main instrument of imperialism we have today neocolonialism.

The essence of neocolonialism is that the State which is subject to it is, in theory, independent and has all the outward trappings of international sovereignty. In reality its economic system and thus its political policy is directed from outside.

...Neo-colonialist control is exercised through economic or monetary means. Control over government policy in the neocolonial State may be secured by payments toward the cost of running the State, by the provision of civil servants in positions where they can dictate policy, and by monetary control over foreign exchange through the imposition of a banking system controlled by the imperial power.

The result of new colonialism is that foreign capital is used for the exploitation rather than for the development of the less developed parts of the world. Investment under neocolonialism increases rather than decreases the gap between the rich and poor countries of the world.

The view has been espoused by many theorists of 'economic underdevelopment.' Nkrumah understood the economics of the colonial question long before most others. He advocated a system he called 'scientific socialism' and indicated how foreign corporations exploited Africa, thereby keeping it from achieving its full potential despite its abundant resources.

Nkrumah envisioned a united Africa at a time when the continent was perhaps not ready. He contended that the colonial powers, even after granting independence, were still controlling the former colonies economically through revolving door loans, aid, unequal trade and exploitation by multinational firms. This was a new concept in Marxist thought – recognizing the former colonies as the proletariat in the Marxist lingo (Smertin, 1990).

Nkrumah argued that African Communalism was 'the social political ancestor of socialism' that had been dislocated by the colonial powers. He concluded by stating that Africans could only move from communalism to socialism...through revolution. It cannot lie through reform. This was the heart of Nkrumahism. Nkrumah was overthrown by a military coup d'etat in 1966 and died in exile. He was one of Africa's greatest economic minds. He represented the voice of the oppressed and exploited masses in Africa, as well as from all over the developing world. Nkrumah viewed colonialism as an economic, rather than a political, phenomenon.

Validity and Critical Analysis of Contributions

Nkrumah's major theories center on the concept of neo-colonialism/imperialism – economic under-development, in a nutshell. Without a doubt, Nkrumah was right about colonial exploitation of Africans by Europeans.

As noted earlier, Nkrumah was more of a politician/statesman than an economist. His theories of imperialism, although valid, in essence stated the obvious. His claim to fame was in bringing the imperialistic nature of foreign governments to light. His theories, however, were essentially a restatement of Marxist-Leninist philosophy.

While an avowed Marxist-Leninist, much like Lenin, Stalin and Mussolini, Nkrumah did not attempt to better the plight of the proletariat in his own country. He was an aristocrat who utilized Machiavellian tactics to retain his position of leadership. Nkrumah also failed to quell the rent-seeking behavior within his own nation. Some historians indicate that Ghana had already attained a high level of development (in comparison to other nations) prior to independence, and that his administration actually arrested Ghana's economic, political and moral development (Omari, 1970). At the height of his rule, Nkrumah was revered as a demi-god.

Nkrumah's insistence on a united Africa is the same unity concept that runs through the African-American community today. He concentrated on uniting Africa and, to a large degree, neglected his own country, Ghana. Nkrumah's contributions to the African continent are exemplary; however, his only contribution to economic theory is that of 'scientific socialism' or 'imperialism' as it relates to Africa. Nkrumah wrote and thought the way he did because those were the times in which he lived. He was an African rising from oppressive colonial rule seeking a solution to the problem. In his eyes, he was the solution.

6 Thomas Sowell – A Neoclassical Thinker (1930-)

All of the economists considered in this study thus far are non-contemporary (are no longer living). We begin in this chapter with the contemporary economists. The first is Thomas Sowell, a Chicago trained neoclassical economist.

Background

Thomas Sowell was born in 1930. He had his humble beginnings in North Carolina and Harlem and was raised in a fairly poor family. He was forced to drop out of high school in the tenth grade because of his family's economic hardship. He eventually entered the military, took advantage of the G.I. bill, and enrolled in night school at Howard University. He left Howard for Harvard, where he graduated in 1958 *magna cum laude* with a degree in economics. Sowell earned his master's degree from Columbia University and his doctorate from the University of Chicago (1968), where he was mentored by Milton Friedman and George Stigler, the Nobel Prize winning economists. Although trained at Chicago, Sowell has not been viewed as a true Chicago economist. His views have been labeled as 'conservative,' a term often applied to black individuals whose views tend to support that of white America. We avoid such labeling in this study. Sowell's views are controversial, especially in the black community. Carl Rowan has described him as 'Ronald Reagan's favorite black intellectual' and as 'Aunt Jemima' giving aid and comfort to America's racists. He has also been hailed by William Saffire as 'one of the brightest men around doing social research' (Bigelow, 1992).

Sowell is a great thinker and researcher, despite his controversial views. We will analyze his career, contributions and views.

Sowell began his economic career as a labor economist with the United States Department of Labor in 1961. He then spent a year as an economics instructor at Douglass College, followed by a year as a lecturer at Howard

University. From 1964 to 1968 Sowell left academics and worked in corporate America as an economic analyst with AT&T. He returned to his Ivy League roots in 1965 as assistant professor at Cornell University, while completing his doctorate at Harvard University. From 1969 to 1972 Sowell was associate professor of economics at Brandeis University and the University of California Los Angeles (UCLA). He then served as project director of the Urban Institute (1972-1974), and a fellow at the Center for Advanced Study in the Behavioral Sciences (1976-1977). He joined the Hoover Institution as fellow in 1977. He returned to the classroom in 1977 as visiting professor of economics at Amherst College and was professor of economics at UCLA from 1974 to 1980. In 1980 he returned to the Hoover Institution at Stanford University as senior fellow, a position he still holds.

Sowell's interests and scholarly contributions are wide-ranging, from history and race relations to pure economics and photography. His views and many writings, although centered around social issues, are in the positivistic vein and are pragmatic in nature. Consequently, Sowell is not as concerned with how fair policies are, but simply whether or not they are effective.

An analysis of Sowell's writings and pronouncements reveal his positive and pragmatic orientation as an economist. Sowell, although a social commentator, is the quintessential positive economist.

Influences

Educated at Chicago, Sowell was influenced by the Chicago School's Milton Friedman, George Stigler, Robert Lucas, and Gary Becker. More importantly, his numerous writings show some evidence of adherence to the tenets of the Chicago School. The tenets that apply include the following (Brue, 1994):

- Optimizing behavior – People attempt to maximize their well-being; they engage in optimizing behavior at the time of their decisions. The basic economic unit is the individual. Individuals combine into larger units to achieve gains.
- Mathematical orientation with an emphasis on empirical verification.
- Self-adjusting nature of the economy with self-limiting minor fluctuations.
- Limited government – Government is inherently inefficient as an agent for achieving objectives that can be achieved through the free market.

Consequently, government may benefit special interests, not the public interest.

Having stated the tenets of the Chicago School, we now turn to Sowell's writings, views and contributions. We analyze his contributions under two broad categories: Positive and Human Capital Theory.

Positive Analysis

Sowell is a positive economist. This adheres to the Chicago School's tenet of empirical investigation and validation. Sowell favors the 'factual' approach to issues. In his many writings he is not overly concerned with what is 'right' or 'wrong,' but prefers to be more pragmatic in applying the test of workability – does a particular policy actually work or does it have the intended effects?

Considered a black dissenter, Sowell writes: 'Most of today's black dissenters, the so-called 'black conservatives,' are scholars whose skills are analytical.' A few examples are in order. Sowell does not favor affirmative action because he believes it has not led to higher incomes for most blacks. The issue is not whether or not affirmative action is fair, just or equitable, but whether or not it has made blacks better off. To resolve this issue, as a true economist, Sowell conducts empirical analyses by marshaling historical data. He concludes, after his study, that affirmative action has not achieved the purpose for which it was designed, that it has not benefited the neediest blacks (those who reside in the ghettos), but that it has been more beneficial to better-off blacks. Moreover, he contends, the statistics suggest that it cannot benefit poor blacks. Sowell's analysis is strictly positive and pragmatic – does it work or not? Ideas to be worthy of acceptance must conform to fact – statistical, social and historical.

Intuitively, Sowell's affirmative action conclusions make sense. It is typically the educated and middle-class blacks who stand to gain from affirmative action policies in hiring, promotions, sub-contracting, and the like. Typically, the poor blacks do not even have the opportunity to take advantage of affirmative action policies. The question is, were affirmative action policies designed for just poor blacks or for all blacks? If the latter is the case, then one may gainsay Sowell's view in spite of his empirical validation.

Another example involves black leadership's view that black political clout has a direct correlation with racial progress. Again, he conducts empirical investigation and discovers that there is a general negative correlation between ethnic political clout and economic progress (Conti, 1993). He concludes that more political clout may not uplift a race. The emphasis, he says, should not be on the political and social but on the economic, as concentration on the former seals the group off from the economy. This is a direct consequence of the limited government tenet. In Sowell's view, more blacks in public office does not ensure black upliftment. He cites examples of black-run cities that have done no better than others.

We contend that most occurrences tend to have multiple causation. It is insular to adhere to a doctrine of single causation. We postulate that political clout may indeed lead to greater economic strength for blacks. Unfortunately, in any capitalist system, the gap between the 'haves' and 'have-nots' tends to grow wider. This is no different in the black community. As blacks have gained political clout, more opportunities have been created; however, not so for poor blacks. This is a capitalistic law, nothing else.

Recalling the tenet of optimizing behavior, we examine Sowell's thoughts on civil rights. Sowell states unequivocally that the civil rights movement has failed. Despite this failure, it continues to receive widespread support. According to Sowell, there is an erroneous public perception that the civil rights leaders have altruistic motives and that their policies are effective. He insists that those responsible for these failed programs be held publicly accountable. He argues in *Knowledge and Decisions* (Sowell, 1980) that most intellectual theorists, bureaucrats, political activists, and civil rights leaders are driven by the self-interest motives; that is, optimizing behavior. Indeed, even intellectuals have the same motivations as everyone else – self-interest. Sowell states, 'Poverty used to be a condition, but now it's an industry. Grants, careers, turf, movements and bureaucratic empires all depend on poverty. With so many vested interests at work, the truth is often buried under a blizzard of rhetoric and myth' (Sowell, 1990). Even though the civil rights intellectuals have not passed the 'test of work ability,' many individuals do not want to criticize them because of political correctness.

In a sense, Sowell is right. However, such criticisms apply to any special group of intellectuals and there is abuse in every system. There are many civil rights leaders who do have almost altruistic motives and many who have made a difference in the lives of poor blacks. Intellectual leadership is needed in all circles for it provides some semblance of hope for the downtrodden. The necessary leadership may spur some to pick themselves up by their own bootstraps. Undoubtedly, civil rights leaders should not be rewarded for simply 'trying to do something.' The efficacy of their projects must be evaluated. In his book *A Conflict of Visions: Ideological Origins of Political Struggle* (1987), Sowell theorizes two visions of existence – the 'constrained' and 'unconstrained.' It is these that lead to social, economic and political clashes. He explains that the unconstrained (leftists) are optimistic believers in increased government involvement to improve society. The constrained (rightists) are realistic and believe in a *laissez-faire* free market system. He denounces the unconstrained vision by stating that people, just by being part of a society, are not entitled to its wealth if they have not made contributions to it.

He has criticized relaxed college admissions, arguing that it can keep people from reaching their full potential and lead to heightened racial tensions. He has also denounced the use of statistical disparities as proof of racial discrimination.

Human Capital Theory

Sowell contends that people are different and that these differences have consequences, some of which are undeniable economic differences. There are real differences in 'human capital' arising from cultural differences between ethnic groups, some of which have historically affected differences in income. In *The Economics of Politics and Race* (1983), he offers several examples.

One such example is that between Irish and Jewish immigrants in America. Although the Irish had political, economic, educational and higher test scores, the Jews were able to surpass the Irish by all standard economic and educational indices (Sowell, 1990). We must not, according to Sowell, dismiss these differences as stereotypical and racist.   The differences are real – both inter- and intra-group.

Sowell further cites an intra-group difference. Using empirical analysis he examined the difference in income between black West Indian immigrants and African-Americans. He discovered that while West Indians earned 94 percent of the United States national average, African-Americans earned only 62 percent of the national average. West Indian 'representation' in the professions was also twice that of African-Americans. Sowell, on this basis, concludes that West Indian human capital, not racial discrimination, is the reason for this disparity.   The West Indian human capital is their skills, frugality and entrepreneurial spirit.

It is worth quoting Lawrence Mead in *The New Politics of Poverty* (1992):

Many immigrants come to America because they want to live an achieving, American-style life, leading to the paradox of immigrants preaching self-reliance to poorer native-born Americans. West Indians typically outstrip native-born blacks, taking jobs that native-born black youths decline due to low pay. In Miami, American-born blacks accuse Cubans and Haitians of truckling to the white man, while the immigrants accuse the natives of lacking the pride to get ahead on their own. 'The Haitians,' confessed a local black psychologist, 'have a sense that we complain too much, that our children are out of control, that we don't do enough for ourselves.'

Undoubtedly, there are intra-group differences and there is some truth to the above statement. On this basis, Sowell challenges the belief that discrimination is the cause of the disparities in income between blacks and whites. Again, he commits the single-causation fallacy. Discrimination, while it affects all blacks, may impact African-Americans even more. African-Americans are a unique group – they are the only group forcibly brought to the United States. This legacy has had a lasting impact. Moreover, West Indians migrate to the United States for a purpose and are, undoubtedly, more driven. Although they may also face discrimination, it is easier for them to overcome because it is not systematized and is not part of their culture from birth. To clarify this point, a 40-year-old West Indian who has been in the United States for ten years only encounters the system for that ten-year period, while a 40-year-old African-American has had to deal with it for 40 years. This systemization creates a difference in culture, manifested (depending on the individual) in human capital.

Indeed, we agree with Sowell that African-Americans must acquire and sustain the necessary human capital to ensure further progress in this economy. Sowell, therefore, stresses the importance of human capital for social mobility. Formal education must stress the basics.

Self Sufficiency Theory

We finally turn to the theory for which Sowell is most known, otherwise known as the 'bootstrap' theory. We attempt to shed more light on his views and dispel some of the erroneous notions surrounding them.

As seen earlier, Sowell has been attacked by the likes of Carl Rowan, Benjamin Hooks, and Julianne Malveaux. We begin our explication with a quote from Sowell himself (Conti, 1993):

> It would be premature at best and presumptuous at worst to attempt to draw sweeping or definitive conclusions from my personal experiences. It would be especially unwarranted to draw Horatio Alger conclusions, that perseverance and/or ability 'win out' despite obstacles. The fact is, I was losing in every way until my life was changed by the Korean War, the draft, and the G.I. Bill – none of which I can take credit for. I have no false modesty about having seized the opportunity and worked to make it pay off, but there is no way to avoid the fact that there first had to be an opportunity to seize.

As seen from this quote, Sowell acknowledges that he received assistance. He in no way implies that he did it all on his own without any help. Sowell's view, often misrepresented, is that once afforded an opportunity, it is up to the individual to muster the personal effort to sustain his/her progress. Sowell believes that while outside help from family mentors and the government may be necessary, they are not sufficient conditions for success. It is up to the individual to initiate and work hard to make progress.

Sowell states that the presence of family and other mediating institutions, such as churches, school and clubs are of extreme importance to individual efforts. In his book *Race and Economics* (1975), he states:

> If the history of American ethnic groups shows anything, it is how large a role has been played by attitudes of self-reliance. The success of the antebellum free persons of color compared to the later black migrants to the North, the advancement of the Italian-Americans beyond the Irish-Americans who had many other advantages, the resilience of the Japanese-Americans despite numerous campaigns of persecution, all emphasize the importance of this factor, however mundane and unfashionable it may be.

He then adds in *The Economics of Politics and Race* (1983):

> The need to form more human capital if prosperity is to be increased is not based on any belief that those who currently possess larger amounts of human capital do so as a matter of personal merit. There is no question that many – perhaps most – of the more fortunate people are recipients of windfall gains they derive from the accident of where they were, if not to immediate affluence, then to families, communities, or nations where the values and patterns of life were a human capital that made economic success more readily obtainable.

These passages indicate that Sowell believes in individual as well as group self-reliance. The family unit is the principle relay station of human capital. It is the family and voluntary organizations, such as churches and clubs, that are to aid the individual, not the government. Attempts must be made to reduce the role of government in individual lives.

Sowell believes welfare hurts black families because it makes them dependent on the government. He investigates this empirically and again says blacks must turn to self-help strategies. The market, he states, has proven it is off over and over again. Succinctly put (Sowell, 1990):

> The 'self-help' approach simply recognizes that blacks do not have unlimited time or resources to put into political crusades, nor are these crusades likely to produce as much net benefit as putting time and resources into developing yourself or your community.

Conclusion

Thomas Sowell has been in ardent opposition to affirmative action for many years. His views on government programs have set the tone for the 'black conservatives' of our time. Typically, so called 'black conservatives' are those who espouse the concept of pulling one's self up by one's own bootstraps. As in most cases, individuals are likely to make extreme arguments. We do not live in an all or nothing world. It is, therefore, possible to take the middle ground and be in favor of some affirmative action. While Sowell recognizes that blacks in America are the only individuals who did not come to these shores of their own free will, he continues to compare them to ethnic groups such as the Irish and Polish-Americans. The background is not the same; the solutions cannot be the same.

Affirmative action programs were designed not for the least qualified, but for the almost-as-qualified, shut-out, and under-represented minorities. These programs allow for those who normally were not afforded opportunities due to discriminatory practices to have access to opportunities that allow them to compete and prove themselves. These programs, in short, even the playing field. Tony Brown provides a most appropriate example when he refers to the National Basketball Association (NBA) draft process. As he puts it, the worst teams are allowed to draft the highest rated or best players to make those teams more competitive – in an attempt to even the playing field. This is, indeed, an appropriate analogy.

No one would argue that affirmative action and quota programs, if abused, would do more harm than good. And to some extent, they have been abused. Should these programs, however, be streamlined and carefully monitored, they can provide those with little opportunity with a competitive advantage.   Relaxed college admissions differ from relaxed graduation requirements. It is not the opportunity to attend college that harms. Being given the opportunity to attend college simply provides students with an opportunity to prove themselves.   In reference to minimum wages, the nonexistence of minimum wage laws would only lead to exploitation of labor, as Marx described it.

Racial discrimination is alive and well. In the absence of laws to reverse discrimination, a permanent underclass would be created. This permanent underclass would at some point be compelled to revolt. We have seen some evidence of this with the Los Angeles riots. It would, therefore, not be these programs that create racial tension, but the lack of them.

Certainly, we all need to pick ourselves up by our own bootstraps. The truth of the matter, however, is that some of us may need just a little push to reach those bootstraps.

From the exposition provided above, it appears that Sowell's views are often misrepresented as too extremist. His views, when placed in perspective and analyzed on a non-emotional basis, appear cogent. There is no need for black intellectuals to label him a pariah for such views, which they appear to misconstrue. Even if they disagree, there is nothing wrong with dissent. Sowell himself wrote (1993):

> Dissenting views are common in every group of people and in every society. A more balanced judgment often emerges out of these clashes of ideas. There is no reason why black Americans must be the only people on this planet who have to skip this process and hit the nail on the head with the first try.

7   Walter E. Williams – Free Enterprise Champion (1936-)

In the early 1980s Walter Williams quipped that he and Thomas Sowell once made a pact never to fly on the same airplane together because a crash would effectively mean the end of black conservatism in America! Indeed, it is through the writings of Williams and Sowell that black conservatism has found a voice. Today, there are many more black conservatives – individuals who advocate more self-help and less dependence on the system.

As with Sowell, Williams is often misunderstood and vilified by other black intellectuals. Black conservatism owes its resurgence after the civil rights movement to these two economists. We use the word 'resurgence' because self-help strategies are not new to the black community. Three of the greatest black leaders of this century – Marcus Garvey, Booker T. Washington and W. E. B. Du Bois – all advocate self-help in one form or another. Since the civil rights movement, however, this concept appears to have become an anathema.

Background and Influences

Williams was born in 1936 in Philadelphia, Pennsylvania. He was raised by his mother, Catherine, who worked as a servant. His father deserted the family when he was only three years old. He attended Philadelphia public schools, and after graduating from high school drove a taxi for two years and served in the United States Army. He obtained his bachelor's degree in economics from California State University in Los Angeles in 1965. He earned a master's degree (1967) and a doctorate (1972) from the University of California in Los Angeles. He served as professor of economics at Temple University from 1973 to 1980. In 1981 he was appointed as John M. Olin Distinguished Professor of Economics at George Mason University in Fairfax, Virginia. He currently holds this position, in addition to serving as chairman of the economics department. He is also adjunct professor of economics at Grove City College in Grove City, Pennsylvania (GMU web site). Williams also served on the faculties of Los Angeles City College (1967-1969) and California State University (1967-1971). From 1963-1967 he served as a group supervisor of juvenile delinquents for the Los Angeles County Probation Department.

Williams is author of numerous publications and is a prolific writer. He has made scores of radio and television appearances, including 'Nightline,' 'Firing Line,' 'Face the Nation,' Milton Friedman's 'Free to Choose,' 'Crossfire,' 'MacNeil/Lehrer Wall Street Week' and many more. Williams writes a weekly syndicated column, which is carried by approximately 160 newspapers, and was a regular commentator for 'Nightly Business Report.' He is also an occasional substitute host for the 'Rush Limbaugh Show.'

Williams has authored six books: *America: A Minority Viewpoint; The State Against Blacks*, which was later made into a PBS documentary entitled 'Good Intentions;' *All It Takes Is Guts: South Africa's War Against Capitalism*, which was later revised for South African publication; *Do the Right Thing: The People's Economist Speaks*; and *More Liberty Means Less Government*.

Williams serves on several boards of directors, including Citizens for a Sound Economy, Reagan Foundation and the Hoover Institution. He serves on advisory boards of Landmark Legal Foundation, Alexis de Tocqueville Institute, Cato Institute and others.

Williams has received numerous fellowships and awards, including the following: Hoover Institution National Fellow, Ford Foundation Fellow, Valley Forge Freedoms Foundation George Washington Medal of Honor, Adam Smith Award, California State University Distinguished Alumnus Award, George Mason University Faculty Member of the Year, and Alpha Kappa Psi Award.

Williams has participated in numerous debates, conferences and lectures in the United States and abroad. He has frequently given expert testimony before Congressional committees on public policy issues ranging from labor policy to taxation and spending. He is a member of the Mont Pelerin Society and the American Economic Association (Walter E. Williams web site).

Williams may be viewed, like Sowell, as a new classicist, some of the tenets of which were outlined in the previous chapter. We will analyze Williams' views by considering his writings on the role of the government and public education.

Role of Government

Williams, like Sowell (although not to the same extent), utilizes positive analysis – economic data and sociological observations – to reach his conclusions. A fierce critic of government intervention, he attributes economic hardship, crime, unemployment and other societal problems to government intervention. According to Williams, government programs have proven deleterious to those they were designed to help.

In the *State Against Blacks* (1982), Williams argues, rather convincingly, that the myriad government social programs have actually impeded black economic progress (Bigelow, 1993). While acknowledging the existence of discrimination and racism, Williams downplays their importance in the ills suffered by blacks. He argues in Sowellian fashion that many of the problems of the black community, such as high crime, teenage pregnancy, illiteracy and high illegitimate birth rates are created, exacerbated and perpetrated by ineffective (albeit well-intentioned) government social programs. The programs have caused many blacks to depend on the system, thereby stifling their desire to achieve. In other words, the giving hurts.

Government programs such as welfare have contributed to the breakdown of the black family. These unearned benefits and subsidies have a dampening effect on the desire to work. Williams is critical of these entitlement programs that provide benefits to homes with single parents and illegitimate children.

Thus, Williams believes, the welfare state fosters behavior that is morally reprehensible and does not allow for the development of strong family values. In the *Christian Science Monitor* (1991), Williams states (Bigelow, 1993):

> We don't have the decency to treat poor people the right way. We do to them what we would never do to someone that we loved. We want to give the poor money without demanding responsibility. Would you do that to your children? If we love our children, we teach them responsibility.

Williams argues that the black community, in the face of greater discrimination four decades ago, was better off in many ways – individuals had higher moral standards, neighborhoods were safer, and communities were more united.

Williams' views and pronouncement are more normative than Sowell's. Williams appears to be more sociologically oriented and is more concerned with prescriptions, not simply analysis. His language is decidedly more value-oriented and subjective. But again, like Sowell, he is misunderstood by the black liberals.

In the new classicist view, Williams champions the free enterprise system, noting that government regulation in many instances prohibits blacks from access to the same opportunities as others. The regulations stifle enterpreneurism by creating certain licensing requirements (cab licenses, etc.) that make it difficult for the 'have-nots' to remain competitive (Bigelow, 1993).

In his 1989 book *South Africa's War Against Capitalism*, Williams states that apartheid was not a result of white owned businesses attempting to exploit black labor (Bigelow, 1993). He posits that the call for separate labor markets was a result of two factors: (1) whites losing their jobs to blacks and (2) whites returning home after World War I to find that they had lost their jobs to blacks. He further argues that divestiture by the international community was much more detrimental to black South Africans because white South Africans were able to purchase these companies at low prices and operate them as they saw fit.

Williams acknowledges the existence of discrimination, yet contends that the problems in the black community are more a result of social programs. He categorically states that blacks are admitted into some colleges in spite of standardized test scores, thus compromising the admissions process. He says this is counter-productive and leads to resentment and bitterness. Williams stands firmly against affirmative action programs. He wrote in *National Review* in 1989 (Bigelow, 1993), 'Official policy calling for unequal treatment by race is morally offensive whether it is applied to favor blacks or applied to favor whites.' He further argues that it is the government's substandard education provided in public schools that leads to poor test scores for blacks. It is not lack of funding, he contends, but monopoly of education by the government that exacerbates the problem. In many instances, teachers get raises and the students are promoted, regardless of ability.

Williams further goes against the grain by arguing against the term 'African-American.' He states that Africa is a continent and not a culture. The tie to Africa is ancestral, not cultural; thus, a better name should be more specific, such as Ghanaian-American, Senegalese-American, Nigerian-American, etc.

Much like Sowell, Williams compares the lack of progress of blacks to other ethnic groups who faced discrimination 40 or 50 years ago and yet have made progress. The government is the culprit. He said on the television program 'Wall Street Week' in 1991, 'All Americans in general, but black

Americans in particular have to recognize that government has always been the enemy; that is, blacks were enslaved because government did not do its job' (Bigelow, 1993).

Conclusion

Williams makes some excellent observations concerning the plight of blacks in the United States. His arguments about the role of government, deterioration of the black community, affirmative action, public education, and the nomenclature of 'African-American' are all considered below.

The most obvious criticism of Williams' arguments is his insistence on single causation. He blames the government for everything without considering other factors that impact black society. Since most occurrences are due to several variables, a multiple causation theory is much more appropriate. Undoubtedly, government's role has had some detrimental effects on blacks, but what about the positives? Racism and slavery have contributed to the plight of blacks in America today. It is extremely unfair to compare blacks to any other group in the United States because all things are not equal; blacks are the only ethnic group forcibly brought to these shores. The institution of slavery has had lasting psychological and economic effects. Affirmative action programs are not necessarily unequal treatment, they simply make the playing field even. They are designed to correct some of the injustices done by the government. This counter-point also applies to college admissions.

Williams' argument concerning public schools creating 'perverse incentives' is valid; however, it does not exonerate the parents and families. The problem begins at home. Families and individuals have to take more responsibility. This counter-argument would also apply to black-on-black crime, drug abuse, etc. Blaming the government will not solve black problems. Whatever happened to individual responsibility? This is where Sowell's views seem more cogent and realistic. Williams is correct in stating that minimum wage laws create unemployment. The theory bears him out; however, in some instances it prevents exploitation of unskilled workers. Williams' argument that sanctions against South Africa hurt South African workers is valid, but again, too insular. The sanctions, to some extent, restricted the free flow of foreign capital to those companies involved in apartheid and exert political pressure, which ordinarily would not have existed, as a catalyst for change. Arguably, without the sanctions, the change would not have come as quickly. Furthermore, some have argued, many South African blacks were so bad off, it was difficult to hurt them further.

Williams' objection to the use of the term 'African-American' for blacks is preposterous. While Africa consists of many cultures and nations, there are nevertheless some homogeneous African cultural concepts, such as respect for one's elders, veneration of ancestors, communalism and the extended family system, to mention but a few. Paradoxically, it would seem that by focusing on the African culture, African-Americans could succeed in lifting the 'yoke of government.'

Finally, while the quality of public school education may indeed be poor, standard monopoly theory does not imply lower quality; it implies lower quantities. Indeed, the government has a monopoly on many public goods (streets, parks, fire service, police service, etc.), yet these are not necessarily of poor quality.

While too much government is bad, we cannot blame all or most of society's ills on government. Government intervention is necessary when done in moderation.

8 Glenn Loury – Self-Help Advocate (1948-)

Like Sowell and Williams, Glenn Loury is another one of those so-called 'conservatives.' In spite of his conservative label, Lowry has not been totally embraced by the conservatives, and is much vilified by the liberals. His views are as interesting, if not more. Loury is an excellent theorist and a profound thinker. He is a true believer in black dignity and self-help. He is also extremely concerned about social issues. We begin our exposition of his views with a look at his background.

Background

Loury was born and raised in the ghettos of South Chicago, Illinois. His grandparents had migrated from rural Mississippi in the years after World War I.

Loury earned a bachelor of arts degree in mathematics from Northwestern University in 1972. He earned his Ph.D. in economics at the Massachusetts Institute of Technology (MIT) in 1976. Already a brilliant mathematics student, Loury decided to apply his quantitative abilities to the area of economics. This was a perfect fit. At MIT, Loury was influenced by the brilliant Nobel Laureates Paul Samuelson and Robert Solow, among others.

After graduating from MIT, Loury returned to his alma mater, Northwestern University, where he served as assistant professor from 1976 to 1979. He joined the faculty at the University of Michigan as associate professor (1979-1980) and as professor (1980-1982). He was then lured to Harvard University where he was professor of economics (1982-1984) and of political economy (1984-1991).

In 1991 he went to Boston University, where he is currently university professor, professor of economics, and director of the Institute on Race and Social Division.

Loury's many scholarly articles include contributions to the fields of welfare economics, game theory, industrial organization, natural resource economics and the economics of income distribution. He has presented his research before numerous scholarly meetings and academic societies throughout the world. He has been a scholar in residence at Oxford University, Tel Aviv University, the University of Stockholm, the Delhi School of Economics and the Institute for Advanced Study at Princeton, and a visiting professor at Institut Fur Die Wissenschaften Vom Menschen. He is a recipient of a Guggenheim Fellowship to support his work.

Loury has served on several advisory commissions for the National Academy of Sciences. He is a fellow of the Econometric Society, and was elected vice president of the American Economic Association for 1997. He was chosen by his Boston University colleagues to present the prestigious University Lecture for the 1996-97 academic year. He has served as a member of the Council on Foreign Relations, and as a fellow of the American Academy of Arts and Sciences.

Loury is also a prominent social critic and public intellectual. His essays on the issues of race, inequality and social policy have appeared in dozens of influential periodicals, including the *New York Times, Wall Street Journal, Washington Post, Commentary Magazine*, and *National Review*. He is a contributing editor at *The New Republic* and a member of the publication committee at *The Public Interest*. He is a frequent commentator on national radio and television, a much sought-after public speaker, and an active advisor on social issues to business and political leaders nationwide. A recent book, *One on One, From the Inside Out: Essays and Reviews on Race and Responsibility in America*, won the 1996 American Book Award and the 1996 Christianity Today Book Award (Boston University web site).

Contributions to the Theory

Loury's contributions are examined by reviewing his theory of human development – social capital and economic upliftment – race relations.

Social Capital (Loury's Theory of Human Development)

Loury's MIT doctoral dissertation was entitled 'Essays in the Theory of Distribution Income.' In the appendix of that dissertation he states, 'Each agent begins life with a random innate endowment. Q is the endowment set, taken to be a subset of an arbitrary, finite dimensional Euclidean space'

(Krugman, 1998). So began his inquiry into the anatomy of race relations and a theory of human development.

In 1981 Loury wrote a paper entitled 'Intergenerational Transfers and the Distribution of Earnings' which appeared in *Econometrica*. In this paper he introduced a model of economic achievement in which an individual's earnings depended on a random endowment of innate ability and skills acquired from formal training. This concept piggybacked on his aforementioned dissertation. His exposition indicated that since people depended on their families to finance their education, their economic opportunities were in large measure a consequence of inherited social position. Consequently, income distribution in each generation depended on the previous generation. As he eloquently states in 'How to Mend Affirmative Action' (Loury, 1997): 'My objective with this model was to illustrate how, in the long-run when people depend on resources available within families to finance their acquisition of skills, economic inequality comes to reflect the inherited advantages of birth. A disparity among persons in economic attainment would bear no necessary connection to differences in their innate abilities.' So, the 'haves' were not necessarily smarter than the 'have-nots.'

In applying this finding to groups, Loury concludes that various societal factors such as race, social class and religion determine a person's choices of association. Furthermore, a person's productivity is not determined solely by innate abilities or full responsiveness to market focus; they depend largely on custom and societal norms (Loury, 1997). He states, 'More concretely, one can say that an adult worker with a given degree of personal efficacy has been 'produced' from the 'inputs' of education, parenting skills, acculturation, nutrition, and socialization to which he was exposed in his formative years.' Undoubtedly, some of those 'inputs' are non-marketable and accrue from society. This is very true as a human development theory. Loury was the first economist to use the term 'social capital' to refer to the role a person's social background plays in their development. In 'A Dynamic Theory of Racial Income Differences' (1977), Loury states:

> Because the creation of a skilled work force is a social process, the meritocratic ideal should take into account that no one travels the road to economic and social success alone. The facts that generations overlap, that much of social life lies outside the reach of public regulation, and that prevailing social affiliations influence the development of the intellectual and personal skills of the young, imply that present patterns of inequality – among individuals and between groups – must embody, to some degree, social and economic disparities that have existed in the past. To the extent that past disparities are illegitimate, the

propriety of the contemporary order is called into question…notwithstanding the establishment of a legal regime of equal opportunity, historically engendered economic differences between racial groups could well persist into the indefinite future. I concluded that the pronounced racial disparities to be observed in American cities are particularly problematic, since they are, at least in part, the product of an unjust history, propagated across the generations by the segmented social structures of our race-conscious society. Thus I would argue, as a matter of social ethics, that the government should undertake policies to mitigate the economic marginality of those languishing in the ghettos of America. This is not a reparations argument. When the developmental prospects of an individual depend on the circumstances of those with whom he is socially affiliated, even a minimal commitment to equality of opportunity requires such a policy. In our divided society, and given our tragic past, this implies that public efforts intended to counter the effects of historical disadvantage among blacks are not only consistent with, but indeed are required by, widely embraced democratic ideals.

In spite of the above, one may be surprised to hear that Loury does not support affirmative action programs that give blacks preferential treatment. Loury believes current affirmative action programs benefit very few blacks, cause resentment, and 'undercut the incentives for blacks to develop their competitive abilities.' Some blacks may actually become underachievers because they are being patronized. There is no pressure for them to work harder. Loury favors programs of a developmental nature, what he terms 'developmental' affirmative action. As he states (Loury, 1997):

Such a targeted effort at performance enhancement among black employees or students is definitely not color-blind behavior. It presumes a direct concern about racial inequality and involves allocating benefits to people on the basis of race. What distinguishes it from preferential hiring or admissions, though, is that it takes seriously the fact of differential performance and seeks to reverse it directly, rather than trying to hide from that fact by setting a different threshold of expectation for the performance of blacks.

For example, given that black students are far scarcer than white and Asian students in the field of math and science, encouraging their entry into these areas without lowering standards – through summer workshops, support for curriculum development at historically black colleges, or the financing of research assistantships for promising graduate students – would be consistent with my distinction between 'preferential' and 'developmental' affirmative action. Also consistent would be the provision of management assistance to new black-owned businesses, which would then be expected to bid competitively for government contracts, or the provisional admission of black students to the state university, conditional on their raising their academic scores to competitive levels after a year or two of study at a local community college. The key is that the racially targeted assistance be short-lived and preparatory to the entry of its recipients into an arena of competition where they would be assessed in the same way as everyone else.

Loury's arguments are cogent and convincing; indeed, they are logical. Unfortunately, the black intellectuals cannot seem to see beyond his criticisms of current affirmative action programs. Fortunately, there are quite a few developmental programs targeted for minorities today, and they appear to be making a difference.

We now turn to Loury's views on economic upliftment.

Economic Upliftment

Loury's concept of economic upliftment focuses on personal responsibility, de-emphasizing racism, recognizing the value of bourgeois norms, emphasizing values and accountability, and the role of the black middle class in serving the underclass.

Loury states unequivocally that black leaders, by continuing to harp on racial animosity and the dire situation of the black underclass, only worsen matters. The victimization theory is ineffective and detrimental to those blacks who need help. He believes, and rightfully so, that blacks should be concerned about the sensibilities of whites and work to gain their respect and assistance in order to make progress. There has been considerable progress made in race relations, and blacks could benefit even more by focusing on reconciliation, not on the rhetoric of oppression and victimization espoused by some black leaders. This does nothing to help poor blacks. He recognizes that most people (including whites) are fair-minded and recognize and respect performance from individuals of every race. Those individuals who are productive will be given kudos, regardless of their color. This point has been proven over and over. Examples abound in sports (Tiger Woods, Michael Jordan), music (Whitney Houston, Puff Daddy), the sciences (George Washington Carver, Ronald McNair), and economics (Sir Arthur Lewis, Andrew Brimmer). Indeed, there needs to be less of a focus on racial disparities and more on individual productivity.

Another way to uplift the black economy, according to Loury, is by recognizing that bourgeois values are by necessity not Eurocentric. Pursuing middle class values is the most effective means of entering the market economy to share the American dream. It is a mistake to denigrate middle class values as 'white' values. There is nothing wrong with anyone aspiring to own a home with a picket fence, and have two and a half children and a dog. He states that social competence is undermined by those values associated with the middle class. Loury also sees a major role for the black middle class in aiding the black poor. This is termed 'communitarianism' by Loury. Succinctly put, those blacks who are prospering are obligated to assist those who are less fortunate. As Loury sees it, the prosperous and bourgeois blacks are beneficiaries of the conditions of the poor blacks.

The various programs designed to serve the underserved are responsible for the successes of many of these individuals; as a consequence, they are obligated to aid their compatriots. As he states (Loury, 1985), '...[the] squalor and hopelessness of the Harlem ghetto [ensures] the legitimacy of preferential treatment for black medical school applicants from Scarsdale.' So even those blacks who are not disadvantaged get a leg up, if you will, due to the plight of those who are. To aid the underclass, it is necessary to harness the talents and 'social capital' of the black middle class. It is the obligation of the black middle class to do what government cannot do. There has to be a joining of hands between the black middle and lower classes in an effort to uplift the latter. This concept is not new. It is very similar to Du Bois' concept of the Talented Tenth. Those individuals who have faired well must offer aid to those who have not.

The obligation of the black middle class goes a step further. It includes the communication of a message of values to the poor. The black leadership must communicate a clear message of the importance of certain middle class values to economic upliftment. According to Loury (1990), self-reliance involves reliance not simply on the individual, but the entire group. He states:

> It makes sense to call for greater self-reliance at this time because some of what needs to be done cannot, in the nature of the case, be undertaken by government. Dealing with behavioral problems, with community values, with the attitudes and beliefs of black youngsters about responsibility, work, family, and schooling is not something government is well suited to do. The teaching of 'oughts' properly belongs in the hands of private, voluntary associations....It is also reasonable to ask those blacks who have benefited from set-asides for black businesses to contribute to the alleviation of suffering of poor blacks, for without the visible ghetto poor, such programs would lack the political support needed for their continuation.

The underclass is hindered by a movement away from values, which for a long time had been an integral part of the black community. Loury believes it is the obligation of black leadership to encourage a return to those values, which include self-sufficiency and family solidarity (Conti, 1993), responsibility, dignity and personal accountability. Loury believes that discrimination and racism still exist, but it is up to blacks to obliterate their own condition. Human beings value dignity, and the victories of the civil rights movement carried with it some amount of dignity. As individuals assume more responsibility for their actions, dignity is affirmed. Blacks must have pride in their achievements and even the poor need to be held accountable for their actions. Poverty should not be directly correlated with a lack of values, morality, dignity or accountability. An example is in order. A poor young black male who has children out of wedlock further worsens his situation and that of others. He is compelled to feed another mouth, pay child support or be incarcerated, all of which affects his earnings potential. The poor woman with whom he had the child is further encumbered because she is not able to pursue her dreams, and the child suffers the consequences. According to Loury, black leadership needs to criticize such behavior, in spite of the political incorrectness of doing so. Even the poor need to realize that there are consequences to their actions for which they must be held accountable. By refusing to address this issue normatively, black leaders are doing the poor a disservice. True dignity requires accountability. Loury said in an interview in 1992 (Conti, 1993):

> There must be a new invigorated movement of self-help in black communities....If people are imbued with a sense of who they are and what their worth is as human beings, then the effect on individuals can outweigh the material incentives. I am not so concerned that welfare has the effect of dulling people's incentives to live in a particular way. I think rather that it is a failure to instill in people an understanding of how they ought to live and to exhibit for them examples of people living in that fashion.

Conclusion

A greater focus on self-reliance, family values, dignity and cooperation would move blacks away from the victimization theory to a point of more self-reliance, accountability, and, over time, economic upliftment. Decrying the evils of racism and discrimination does not move blacks any further ahead. Loury's views on human capital and black economic development are well founded and justified. Instead of misconstruing and misreading his views, black leadership needs to give them serious consideration.

9 William Darity, Jr. – Contemporary Ethnic Researcher (1953-)

William Darity, Jr. is another notable economist who could be considered a mainstreamer. Although less prominent than the last three contemporaries, his research is equally significant.

Background

Darity was born in 1953 in Flat Rock, North Carolina. He obtained a Ph.D. in economics from the Massachusetts Institute of Technology in 1978. In 1999 he joined the Duke faculty half time as research professor of public policy studies. He currently serves as Cary C. Boshamer professor of economics at the University of North Carolina (UNC) at Chapel Hill. He also holds an appointment as research professor of public policy, African and African American studies and economics at Duke University. At UNC he has served as director of the Minority Undergraduate Research Assistant Program, director of the Undergraduate Honors Program and director of Graduate Studies. He was a fellow at the National Humanities Center (1980-90) and a visiting scholar at the Federal Reserve's Board of Governors (1984). He also taught economics at the Centro de Excelencia Empresarial (Monterrey, Mexico), Grinnell College, the University of Tulsa, the University of Texas at Austin, the University of Maryland at College Park, and Simmons College.

Darity's research focuses on inequality by race, class and ethnicity, North-South theories of development and trade, history of economic thought and political economy, the Atlantic slave trade and the Industrial Revolution, and social psychology effects of unemployment exposure.

He is the co-author of *Persistent Disparity: Race and Economic Inequality in the United States Since 1945* (1998) and *The Black Underclass: Critical Essays on Race and Unwantedness* (1994). He also co-authored

Macroeconomics (1994); 'Racial Earnings Disparities and Family Structure,' *Southern Economic Journal* (1998); 'Evidence on Discrimination in Employment: Codes of Color, Codes of Gender,' *Journal of Economic Perspectives* (1998); 'Secular Changes in the Gender Composition of Employment and Growth Dynamics in the North and the South,' *World Development* (2000); 'Racial and Ethnic Economic Inequality: The International Record,' *AER* (2000); and 'Tracing the Divide: Intergroup Disparity Across Countries,' *Eastern Economic Journal* (2000). He is the editor of *Economics and Discrimination* (2 volumes, 1995), and the author of *The Loan Pushers: The Role of Commercial Banks in the International Debt Crisis* (1988) and 'Keynes, Employment Policy and the Underclass' in *Improving the Global Economy: Keynesianism and the Growth in Output and Employment* (1997).

Human Capital

Darity's research has focused on various dimensions of economic inequality – between the sexes, races, ethnic groups, regions, and nations. He has written numerous articles, conducted research projects, developed models, and continues to conduct research on the subject.

Most of Darity's writings are positive in nature. His research is empirical and he tends not to dwell on the normative.

In the November 1995 issue of *World Development*, Darity develops a model incorporating gender into a household model for sub-Saharan Africa. This is the first model of its kind applied to developing countries. A 1997 article by Campbell and Warner suggests that the model could be improved by including additional assumptions involving the woman's ability to bargain and work/leisure substitution. In spite of its shortcomings, however, it has important implications for policy makers in the developing world.

Darity, in another article (1993), concludes after much empirical analysis that, contrary to Sowell's conclusions, the higher success rates of West Indian immigrants and Jews is due to the selective immigration of middle class representatives of those groups, not because their cultures differ from African-Americans. He concludes that the split-labor market theory is the major reason for racial income inequality in the United States.

Darity here commits the same error as Sowell – the error of single causation. No one would doubt that there is some merit in his theory, but there is the possibility of variables other than class background, such as cultural differences.

Continuing with his analysis of race and earnings, Darity co-authored a series of papers with David Guilkey and William Winfrey (1995). They apply Blinder-Oaxaca decompositions and ordinary least squares (OLS) methods to 1980 and 1990 census data on race and gender. They conclude that inter-ethnic earnings disparities are much greater in the male population than it is in the female population. For example, white men of Russian ancestry earned 150 percent of the male average income; black men earned only 62 percent. This difference, they say, is not only due to differences in educational attainment: 'Obviously a given human capital endowment is not converted into earnings at the same rate for members of each group.' In their own words (Darity, et. al, 1995):

> First, we desegregated the black male population into different ancestral/cultural groups: West Indian, non-West Indian Hispanic, European and a group of all others who constitute 'native' blacks, primarily descendants of North American slaves. Results show that for men the discrimination result holds up regardless of the cultural group. Second we desegregated the Hispanic male population into black and non-black subgroups. Although both groups are discriminated against, the black group is discriminated against to a much larger extent. Thus when we control for color the degree of discrimination was high across all of the groups. When we control for culture the degree of discrimination changed sharply with color. Our preliminary conclusion is that color, i.e., racial discrimination, is more important than culture in explaining outcomes for males.

Darity continues to conduct empirical research showing that discrimination negatively impacts minority groups. Unlike Sowell, Williams and Loury, he provides little normative analysis. Consequently, it is worth adding here that the data shows in no uncertain terms that in spite of discrimination, those groups whose earnings lag behind tend to be the least educated. For example, Russian men had 3.75 years of college in 1990 while black men had only .91 years. Even in the absence of discrimination, one would conclude that Russian men ought to earn more than blacks. Again and again, in spite of all the conflicting arguments, it boils down to one fact – the development of human capital. Education is the key!

Darity's research tends to be positive in nature. As the youngest of the contemporary economists in this study, his research is path breaking and will continue to impact race research issues for years to come.

10 Andrew F. Brimmer – The Business Consultant (1926-)

In the last four chapters we provided the views of four remarkable and controversial contemporary black economic theorists. In the next three we provide expositions of the views of three other economists who are less controversial and, consequently, more mainstream, but no less remarkable. We begin with perhaps the best known of the three – Andrew Brimmer.

Background

Andrew Brimmer was born in 1926 to a sharecropper father and warehouse-working mother in rural northeast Louisiana. He picked cotton as a child growing up along the Mississippi River. Despite coming from an indigent family, his upbringing was one of self-confidence, high values, and high standards. Brimmer persevered in his studies and was able to earn bachelor's and master's degrees in economics from the University of Washington in Seattle. He earned his Ph.D. in economics at Harvard University in 1957.

Brimmer was the first African-American to be named a governor of the Federal Reserve System. He served in that position from 1966 to 1974.

Brimmer is considered one of the foremost leading African-American economic theorists today. Currently, he is president of his own economic consulting firm in Washington, DC, and serves as vice-president of the Commodity Exchange. He is a leading monetary theorist as well as a leading figure in the world banking system, especially as it relates to Third World economies. It would seem that as one who has lived in a developing nation (he earned a Fulbright to India in 1951 and published several articles on the Indian economy) and as one of African ancestry, Brimmer is certainly in tune with the problems of the Third World.

Brimmer has served in numerous positions, including the following: economist, Federal Reserve Bank of New York; assistant professor of economics, Michigan State University and University of Pennsylvania; consultant to the Security Exchange Commission; deputy assistant

79

secretary and assistant secretary for economic affairs, Department of Commerce; governor of the Federal Reserve Board; visiting professor, Harvard University; president, Brimmer and Company Consulting; and board member of several organizations and corporations.

Brimmer is former chairman of the District of Columbia Financial Responsibility and Management Assistance Authority. He is also director of several corporations, including Black Rock Mutual Funds, and is a former director of Bank of America, DuPont, and UAL (United Airlines).

Brimmer's research is focused mainly in the area of monetary policy, international finance, and capital markets. His extensive publications include *International Banking and Domestic Economic Policies: Perspectives in Debt and Development* (1986); co-chairman, *Origins and Causes of the S&L Debacle: A Blueprint for Reform*, National Commission on Financial Institution Reform, Recovery & Enforcement (1993); 'Central Banking and Systemic Risks in Capital Markets,' *The Journal of Economic Perspectives* (1989); 'Financial Regulation and the Fragility of the Banking System,' *North American Journal of Economics & Finance* (1998); and 'Economic Cost of Discrimination Against Black Americans,' in Margaret C. Simms, editor: *Economic Perspectives on Affirmative Action*, Joint Center for Political and Economic Studies (1995).

Additional books include *The Setting of Entrepreneurship in India* (1955); *Some Studies in Monetary Policy; Interest Rates and Investment Behavior of Life Insurance Companies* (1957); and *Life Insurance Companies in the Capital Market* (1962). He has written numerous articles and made contributions to *Black Enterprise, Ebony, Jet, New York Times*, and *The New York Magazine*, among others. He is the most prominent living black economist.

As indicated earlier, Brimmer's focus is on the monetary system, Third World economies, and the black economic condition. He is against viewing the problems of the Third World debt in general terms. He states (Bigelow, 1992):

> Different countries face a variety of particular obstacles which arise from specific circumstances related to their respective economies. Consequently, it would not only be futile but harmful as well to attempt to mandate a common, universal solution to the debt problem plaguing developing countries.

He has through a series of articles and lectures discussed topics and propounded solutions to the economic problems of blacks. He has written on the economic cost of discrimination and the cost of bank bias. Invariably, Brimmer concludes that discrimination imposes additional costs not only on those discriminated against, but on society as a whole. He argues that discrimination in employment lowered the gross domestic product (GDP) by 1.5 percent to 2.2 percent during the past 25 years, due to a combination of not making full use of African-American educational achievement and failure to improve educational levels. In 1991 alone, he states, this amounted to a $215 billion loss in GDP (Brimmer, 1992).

He has also studied statistics indicating that personal income in suburban areas increase after an African-American is elected mayor, while personal income in cities decrease due to high regulations (Brimmer, 1992). Although he decries discrimination, he argues that it is not the only variable in the equation of black problems.

On Banking and Debt

Brimmer is an acknowledged expert on economic development, especially as it applies to sub-Saharan Africa. It is difficult to classify Brimmer as anything but a monetary economist. Although there is no separate school of monetary economics (it is neo-classical), the emphasis on money growth spurring the economy pervades his views.

Brimmer has written numerous articles on black banks. We analyze his views here by focusing on his article entitled 'The Dilemma of Black Banking: Lending Risks vs. Community Service' (1992).

Brimmer conducts empirical analysis and concludes that black-owned banks face a serious dilemma. As these banks attempt to supply credit, they face the exceptional risks of lending to communities with lower incomes and higher rates of bankruptcy. As they try to meet the needs of these communities, their rate of failure increases. Brimmer marshals data detailing the banks, locations, assets, and period of black ownership. He concludes that black-owned banks often assume high risk, coupled with the insensitive policies of federal bank supervisors. Consequently, while they may exhibit missionary zeal in serving the black community, they must as a matter of survival exercise restraint in lending. If these banks fail, it further puts their depositors, debtors and creditors at risk. Lack of restraint by these banks, although they mean well, may be deleterious to the black communities they serve.

Brimmer is one of the least controversial and more mainstream of the economists included in this study. His view of the Third World debt problem is, to a large degree, valid. The debts of the various nations may have arisen from specific policies for which a panacea cannot be prescribed. However, in most instances, these problems are the result of the same ills – poor management by the leaders coupled with corruption and ineffective policies. Each nation, however, needs to be viewed independently. These nations are, nonetheless, responsible in many instances for their own maladies.

His argument on the cost of discrimination against blacks and other minority groups is veracious. Discrimination leads to inefficiency in the sense that productive resources are underutilized, leading to losses in productivity. Brimmer correctly recognizes that discrimination is only one of the variables in the equation of black problems. In this sense, Brimmer is less critical of the system than black intellectuals such as Sowell and Williams. He has conducted many path-breaking studies, and is a pioneer in the purest sense of the word.

On Black Wealth and Income

Brimmer is perhaps the most complete contemporary evaluator of the economic condition of blacks. He utilizes empirical analysis to reach his conclusions. Brimmer utilizes data and actual observations to analyze the condition of black businesses. A number of his publications center around the issue of the black condition, especially in business and employment.

We focus here on Brimmer's analysis of black business and the black economy. We analyze Brimmer's contributions by reviewing two of his articles, '45 Years in Business and Employment' (1990) and 'Long-term Trends and Prospects for Black-Owned Businesses' (1998).

Brimmer analyzes the state of black economy over the past four decades from 1960 to 1990. He concludes that even though participation by blacks in the labor force rose, they suffered a sizable job deficit. In spite of this, black unemployment in 1990 was still more than twice that of whites. Partially responsible for this situation, according to Brimmer, is racial discrimination. He, however, notes that the lack of skills or human capital was a major part of this equation. Those blacks who possessed education and the necessary skills continued to make progress. Here, Brimmer, like Sowell and Williams, places a premium on education. No one can over-emphasize the importance of education for any group of people. It is the key to overcoming a number of obstacles.

Brimmer noted that many black men had dropped out of the workforce; consequently, black women were contributing more economic support to black families. The income deficit for blacks decreased between 1947 and 1989 by over 16 percent. Increasingly, the gap between rich and poor blacks has widened more than that between whites. This again points to the fact that those blacks with fewer marketable skills continue to fare worse. He notes that the area of technology is an area that blacks need to consider. The deficits in employment and income were also reflected in wealth accumulation.

In the area of wealth accumulation, there is a greater shortfall for blacks. He concludes (1990):

> To a major degree, the deficit in wealth accumulation is traceable to the long history of deprivation which blacks have suffered in the Untied States. They have had fewer opportunities than whites to earn, to save, to accumulate wealth, and to pass that wealth on to their children.

The above statement is undoubtedly true. To paraphrase President Lyndon B. Johnson, we cannot expect an athlete who has had little or no training to be as competitive as one who has trained his entire life. This is the basis of affirmative action.

On Black Business Ownership

In the two articles referenced above, Brimmer evaluates the state of black businesses from 1940 to 1990. Brimmer concedes that from 1940 to 1980 black business ownership declined. He draws a parallel between the nature of black businesses and protective tariffs, noting that these businesses fared well initially because they had a monopoly on black consumers. He writes (Brimmer, 1990):

> Historically, Black-owned firms grew up behind a wall of racial segregation and discrimination which served as a kind of protective tariff. Many White-owned businesses refused to serve Blacks or did so on a segregated basis. This was especially true of personal services and public accommodations. Because of this exclusion, Black businessmen and women had an opportunity to respond to the unmet needs. They provided the barber and beauty shops (and produced the cosmetics as well). They operated the hotels, restaurants, and local retail stores. Since major insurance companies refused to sell policies to Blacks – or did so on a discriminatory basis – Black life insurance companies developed.
>
> However, with the decline of racial segregation – particularly after the passage of the Civil Rights Act of 1964 – the protective tariff for Black-owned businesses eroded rapidly. Their markets shrank at a time when the purchasing power of the Black community was expanding noticeably. As their incomes

rose, many Black consumers expanded their demand for goods and services which Black firms could not provide. Many Blacks also moved to different parts of cities or to the suburbs – while most Black firms remained behind in the older, segregated neighborhoods. Moreover, many nationwide manufacturers, retailers, and financial institutions began to recognize the potentials of the Black consumer market, and this competition had a severely negative impact on Black-owned businesses.

Essentially, black businesses are now compelled to compete with major conglomerates for the black customers to whom they formally had exclusive access. In order for black businesses to survive, they must diversify and serve a wider clientele beyond the black community. Black firms must strategize and focus on a wider appeal, both nationally and internationally. In order to survive well into the twenty-first century, a global and multi-cultural emphasis is imperative.

The Disparity Index

In his article entitled 'Long-Term Trends and Prospects for Black-Owned Business' (1998), Brimmer develops a disparity index for black-owned businesses. Brimmer continues his empirical analysis of the black economy from the mid-1980s to the early 1990s. He provides data on the growth of black-owned businesses, business sales and black income, industry distribution of sales, and sectoral information on black businesses.

He indicates that in the 1990s, the amount of income from black households going to black businesses increased slightly due to the following: (1) diversification to better meet black demands, (2) following blacks to the suburbs, and (3) expanding their participation in the economy at large.

Brimmer calculates a Disparity Index (DI), which is a broad gauge of black participation by black firms. The DI is calculated as follows:

$$DI = \frac{S_b}{S_t} + \frac{N_b}{N_t} \times 100,$$

Where:
   S_b = Sales of black firms
   S_t = Sales of all firms
   N_b = Number of black firms
   N_t = Number of all firms

If the DI is equal to 100.00, blacks' share of total sales matches their share of total firms in an industry. This ratio indicates that blacks' market access is unimpeded. If the DI reading is below 100.00, it implies that blacks are excluded from full participation. To some extent, the latter may be due to discrimination. A DI above 100.00 suggests that blacks enjoy special advantages in the particular industry.

Provided in Table 10.1 below are Brimmer's calculations for ten broad industry groups between 1987 and 1992.

Table 10.1 **Changes in Disparity Indexes for Black-Owned Businesses, 1987-92**

Industry	1987	1992	Change: 1987-92 (Percentage Points)
All industries	32.01	26.92	-5.09
Agriculture	53.75	38.67	-15.08
Mining	43.34	49.03	5.69
Construction	41.77	36.72	-5.05
Manufacturing	24.41	15.12	-9.29
Transportation & PU	33.02	27.40	-5.62
Wholesale Trade	32.55	30.87	-1.68
Retail Trade	36.71	27.46	-9.25
Fin., Ins., R.E.	29.55	56.87	27.32
Services	41.48	39.08	-2.40
Other Industries	37.55	57.37	19.82

Source: Calculations by Brimmer & Company, Inc. Review of Black Political Economy, 1998.

The findings suggest that all DIs were considerably below par in all sectors. There were improvements in some areas and declines in others. Some improvements were due to affirmative action programs, however, there were concerns in all areas.

Brimmer concludes that in order for more progress to occur, blacks will have to focus on technology and provide services outside the black community. Black businesses, to survive, must focus on being more inclusive.

11 Phyllis Ann Wallace – A Female Pioneer (1920?-1993)

Phyllis Ann Wallace is the lone female in this study. This is not to say that there are no other prominent black female economists. While there are some, she is the most noteworthy. Wallace died in 1993. Her work focused primarily on the labor market and occupational trends; consequently, we view her as a labor economist. She was concerned both with the plight of women in the labor market and the plight of black women. She covered topics ranging from affirmative action to collective bargaining and employment patterns in the pharmaceutical industry.

Background

Wallace was born in Baltimore, Maryland and graduated from Baltimore's Frederick Douglass High School. She was barred from attending the University of Maryland due to her race. Because her chosen field of study was not offered at historically black Morgan State University, she obtained a degree in economics at New York University (NYU), graduating *magna cum laude* and Phi Beta Kappa. Wallace went on to Yale University where she earned her master's and doctoral degrees in 1944 and 1948, respectively. She was perhaps the first black to receive a Ph.D. in economics from Yale, and was the first black female to do so.

Wallace's positions have been in research and government agencies as well as academic institutions. Some of her positions include economics lecturer, City College of New York; researcher, National Bureau of Economics Research; policy analyst, Central Intelligence Agency; vice president, Metropolitan Applied Research Center; economics professor, Atlanta University; chief of technical studies, Equal Employment Opportunity Commission; and professor of economics, Massachusetts Institute of Technology.

Wallace enjoyed a distinguished career in teaching, research and government service.

86

Upon graduation from Yale, Wallace was offered an economic analyst position with the National Bureau of Economic Research, where she focused on international trade. From 1948 to 1952 she was also an instructor at the City College of New York. In 1953 she left New York and joined the faculty of Atlanta University as an associate professor.

She left Atlanta University in 1957 to take a position as a government economist with the Central Intelligence Agency (CIA). While with the CIA, she specialized on the Soviet economy and co-authored a paper entitled 'Industrial Growth in the Soviet Union,' which was published in the *American Economic Review* (1959). Malveaux (1994) indicates that Wallace's years in intelligence kept her isolated. In 1965, soon after the Civil Rights Act, Wallace was invited to join the newly formed Equal Employment Opportunity Commission (EEOC) as director of technical studies. This is when she began to study the economics of discrimination among African-Americans and women in the workforce.

In 1968 Wallace left the EEOC to work for the Metropolitan Applied Research Center (MARC), where she focused on research on urban youth. She published extensively during this time. In 1972 she was invited to join the Massachusetts Institute of Technology (MIT) as a visiting professor. She was tenured as a full professor in 1974, and became the first black professor at MIT.

At MIT, Wallace continued her research on minorities and designed programs to recruit more black students. Some of these students included Glenn Loury, William Darity (two of the notable economists included in this study), and Julienne Malveaux, among others. During her career Wallace won many accolades and served on many boards.

Economics of Discrimination

As part of the EEOC, Wallace began her efforts to address issues of discrimination by taking a new approach to social research and implementing new methodologies. Building teams of workers from different professions, she gathered lawyers, economists, and even psychologists to study individual cases. Much of Wallace's work culminated in the early 1970s when she directed the research for the federal lawsuit charging the largest private employer in the United States, AT&T, with sexual and racial discrimination. The 1973 decision found the company guilty of the charges, and led to significant changes in employment practices (Mabunda, 1995).

Among her most powerful work is her book *MBAs on the Fast Track* (1989). A longitudinal study of Sloan School graduates that was completed only through painstaking research, the study shows gaps between men's and women's pay, and between the pay of black and white MBAs. Wallace was also able to document trends that only recently have been distilled into contemporary jargon. 'Dinks' (double incomes, no kids), 'glass ceilings,' and commuter marriages were all trends that she captured in the early days of compiling her data (Malveaux, 1994). In 1974 Wallace conducted research on teenagers.

Wallace's research reflected her opinions. She began to report the unpopular statistics on blacks in the economy and to change the way the data was collected and analyzed. Until her pioneering studies, researchers in the area focused primarily on married black women in comparison to married white women, which led to misleading results. In her book *Black Women in the Labor Force* (1980), Wallace pointed out that almost fifty percent of all black families were headed by single black women and, thus, the traditional approach to research neglected much of the population. Judith Wilson reported in a review in *Essence* that the book '[took] the first step toward changing techniques used to gather research data on black women by demonstrating the need for a more effective research methodology, one based upon our specific needs and realities' (Mabunda, 1995).

One of those realities was the long-term ineffectiveness of the Equal Opportunity Act of 1972 and earlier government programs set up to aid minority workers. Wallace wrote in an article in *Black Enterprise* that while 'the Manpower programs of the 1960s attempted to enhance the employability of many minority workers who had been restricted to a peripheral role in the labor market, these programs appear not to have had a lasting effect on the relative employment and earnings position of blacks.' Many of the gains made by black workers in the 1960s were nullified in the recession of the early 1970s, which caused layoffs of new workers with low seniority. Thus, Wallace concluded, 'after more than a decade of implementation of laws and regulations prohibiting racial discrimination in employment, discrimination in the work place is still pervasive' (Mabunda, 1995).

On Human Capital

Wallace saw barriers to the advancement of women in international markets. The solution was to have more employment training programs. This would ensure that the United States would maintain its competitive edge in the world economy. The continuous development of human capital would be key to the information technology markets. This human capital development was to be made available to all, especially the most disadvantaged, as it would make them and the entire nation more competitive.

Conclusion

Wallace was a pioneer and made a variety of contributions to economics. Her most noteworthy contributions have been in the areas of workplace discrimination (race and gender). Wallace published numerous books and articles. Some of her works include *Pathways to Work; Unemployment Among Black Teenage Females* (1974); *Women, Minorities, and Employment Discrimination* (1977); *Black Women in the Labor Force* (1980); *Women in the Workplace* (editor, 1982); and *MBAs on the Fast Track* (1989).

Wallace made key contributions in the areas of research on the status of African-Americans in urban poverty neighborhoods and on patterns of employment in the private sector. She also developed interdisciplinary teams that focused on issues of discrimination and employment testing. She was the first scholar to focus on issues affecting young black women in the workplace. This is documented in her book *Black Women in the Labor Force* (1980). In this book she focuses on a group that few had paid attention to prior to that period, and provides documentation on the various roles played by black women in the workplace. She states that this group had, up until that point, been lumped either with blacks in general or with white women, and noted that their characteristics warranted their being considered separately. This book challenged the myths about these women's employment aspirations and brought to light the enormous discrimination they encountered while seeking white-collar employment (Malveaux, 1994).

In her book *MBAs on the Fast Track* (1989), Wallace studied MBA graduates from MIT and discovered disparities in pay based on gender as well as race. She documented trends such as commuter marriages and the concept of the 'glass ceiling.'

Wallace became the first African-American and the first woman president of the Industrial Relations Research Association. She noted that training and employment programs for women and minorities would serve as a catalyst in ensuring that the economy of the United States remained competitive globally. In addition to her many accomplishments, Wallace also served as president of the American Economic Association. While at the EEOC, she pioneered the use of occupational employment data (Malveaux, 1994).

She was a pioneer who made many contributions to the economic profession, black community, and the nation as a whole. Her greatest contributions were in the area of employment discrimination based on race and gender. Prior to her path-breaking studies on black women in the work force, no one had thought enough of this group to consider it separately. As Malveaux (1994) states, the theme of Wallace's academic and civic work is 'tilting against the wind, shattering stereotypes, choosing the road less traveled.'

12 Clifton R. Wharton, Jr. – A Trailblazer (1926-)

Clifton R. Wharton, Jr. has been referred to as a trailblazer; however, this is an understatement. He has achieved an incredible number of black firsts – first African-American to receive a Ph.D. in economics from the University of Chicago, the first to head a Fortune 100 company, the first to head New York State's Public University System, and the first deputy secretary of state.

Wharton is a true pioneer leader and scholar. His views may also be considered mainstream. We examine his life and views here by referring to some of his speeches and writings.

Background

Wharton was born in Boston, Massachusetts. He spent many years of his youth in the Canary Islands where his father was stationed as a United States foreign service officer. He attended Boston Latin High School and Harvard University. Upon graduation from Harvard, he obtained a master's degree from the School of Advanced International Studies at Johns Hopkins University. He was the first black student to do so. He later attended the University of Chicago where he earned another master's degree and a doctorate in economics. He again was the first black to do so.

Wharton's positions have been in the corporate as well as academic world. He has achieved numerous firsts. He was the first African-American in this country to head a predominantly white university (Michigan State, 1970-78). He also became the first African-American to head a Fortune 100 company when he was selected as CEO of the Teachers Insurance and Annuity Association and the College Retirement Equities Fund (TIAA-CREF). In addition, Wharton has held numerous positions, which include director of operations in Southeast Asia and vice president for the Agricultural Development Council (ADC); chancellor of the State University of New York; and deputy secretary of state for the United States Department of State (another first).

Wharton is an international economist, academic, and political administrator. Perhaps of all the economists included in this study, he has made the fewest contributions to the theory. Unlike many of the others, Wharton has not proposed any major economic theories. It is his training as an economist – the first African-American to earn a Ph.D. in economics from the University of Chicago – and his business and managerial acumen that set him apart from the rest.

Wharton has contributed to numerous professional journals and has authored or edited books, including the following: *Subsistence Agriculture and Economic Development* (editor); *Continuity and Change: Academic Greatness Under Stress*; and *Patterns for Lifelong Learning* (with Theodore M. Hesburg).

Wharton focused on world development issues, with his work centering on Latin America. Through his work with the Agricultural Development Council (ADC) in Southeast Asia, he became an expert in agrarian reform, realizing that nations could achieve measurable levels of economic growth by focusing on maintaining a threshold standard of living through subsistence farming.

As president of Michigan State University, he handled the student riots effectively. A new building on campus was named in his honor following his eight-year tenure. In 1978 he became chancellor of the State University of New York (SUNY). This system had 64 campuses, a $2.5 billion budget, 70,000 employees, and hundreds of thousands of students. The system was ailing and failing. He succeeded in utilizing his skills and training as an economist to turn the system around.

Wharton's tenure as president of TIAA-CREF led to a doubling of the pension fund's assets to $113 billion. In 1993 Wharton was appointed to the second highest-ranking position at the United States Department of State. Nine months later he resigned this position (Bigelow, 1994).

For Wharton, his color was never an excuse. In terms of economics, however, Wharton's contributions have been primarily in economic development. The concept of economic development through subsistence agriculture is not new, and Wharton has made few economic pronouncements. He is, nevertheless, an economic pioneer.

On Economic Development and Aid

Wharton edited a text on the role of subsistence agriculture and economic development (Wharton, 1969). The general theme of this text is that subsistence agriculture, when practiced properly, ensures that the masses are fed. It is the surplus that spurs economic growth.

Wharton's involvement with economic development goes as far back as his days with Nelson Rockefeller's technical assistance programs in Latin America. He referred to this in a statement before the Foreign Relations Committee (Wharton, 1993). He stresses his commitment to foreign aid, because many of the conflicts around the world result from economic stress and injustice. As he states, 'To the extent that instability results from poverty, inequality of political and economic access, and societal transformation – as it often does – effective development assistance helps reduce tensions that breed violent conflict.' It is the role, therefore, of those nations that can to support those less fortunate, for all these nations are linked in an expansive global economy. He further testifies:

> The challenge is to contribute to a growing, prosperous international economy while rebuilding our own at home. Emerging economies represent tremendous potential growth and new markets. Participating in their growth expands the market for our goods through trade and investment. It also creates U.S. jobs, enhances the supply of consumable goods, and improves the flow of strategic material...'winning' this battle need not be a zero-sum game; assisting economies to thrive abroad promotes peace, jobs, stabilization, a demand for U.S. products and services, and higher living standards for all.

The United States is, therefore, compelled to expand its participation in the international economy. He adds that it is important that the United States work to foster democratic ideals worldwide since 'economic development works best in participatory democracies.' It is the role of the United States to ensure that we do not return to the days of isolationism and mercantilism. He calls for the United States to exercise 'compassion, enlightened self-interest, a willingness to share, and a deep respect for the human dignity of all people.' These must be the basis of United States foreign aid. From these statements to the Foreign Relations Committee, it is obvious that Wharton is aware of the exploitative nature of some of the policies of the United States. Because of his twenty-two years of professional foreign experience in Latin America and Asia, he can sympathize and empathize with the inhabitants of the developing world. There is a human variable that he remains cognizant of. He calls for addressing environmental concerns in order to reduce the negative impacts of one nation's actions on its neighbors. In this sense, Wharton may be viewed as a welfare economist. He is concerned with the maximization of social well being in a global sense. He is also concerned about population growth, high fertility rates, health issues, and migration of refugees. In the quest to aid the international 'have-nots,' he tells the Foreign Relations Committee (1993):

> With the end of the Cold War, promoting sustainable development has become a more prominent national objective, bridging domestic and foreign policy. The major commitment to assist the development of democracy and a market economy is just as valid in a Russia and a Guatemala as it is in a Haiti and a Cambodia. USAID's mix of policy recommendations and technical assistance will be different for the traditional developing countries compared with our more advanced partners, but the overarching goal of engaging them in an expanding global market economy will be the same.

Human Capital and Values

Wharton's views on human capital and values are expounded in a speech he gave while director of the New York Stock Exchange (Wharton, 1999). Wharton believes that economic gain plays a vital role in motivating economic behavior. No ethnic group is more or less motivated by greed than another. Consequently, no group's values are more responsible for their successes than another. This is another view in direct opposition to Sowell's. Wharton does, however, indicate that even if there were value differences, the traditional economic forces are still predominant. The key to success, he says are education and human capital. He cites empirical research to support his thesis. According to Wharton, emphasis needs to be placed on the development of human capital, especially in the high technology area. He states that any strategy to capture 'advances in knowledge' must never forget its fundamental origin (Wharton, 1995). I am referring to the human dimension, the human capital, which is the ultimate source of growth and the resource for creating new knowledge. Human capital is the magic key underlying this entire process.

The global explosion in knowledge and the technological skills to access and use that knowledge have become pivotal factors in determining individual social and economic viability in virtually every country around the globe. The old axiom that knowledge is power was never more true. Future careers and incomes are often predetermined by the quality and content of the education received – the build up in one's human capital. The greater the investment and build up in personal intellectual capital, the greater the financial rewards. In the United States, for example, a person with a college degree earns 72 percent more than a high school graduate, and someone with an advanced degree earns 162 percent more.

Wharton cautions that an effort must be made to share all societal gains with the masses. In his pronouncements he shows his genuine humanitarianism by not losing sight of the masses. This is reflected in the following two statements:

There is another dimension of human capital and the growth in knowledge that is significant for future economic growth. Earlier I noted that an important strategy in global competition is to develop indigenous technology through research based upon the knowledge and expertise of its own human capital. However the technology is obtained, whether domestically or from abroad, it is vital that its benefits be shared widely with the men and women of the labor force in order to improve their standard of living. Their health, vigor, and intelligence invariably will play a critical role in any sustained economic development. Such an emphasis will help create a powerful, lasting economic force in its own right....Yes, advances in knowledge and technology are a boon with the potential for increasing the growth and income levels of more and more nations, but it is merely a tool, not a solution. Only if used wisely and with broad participation in its benefits, will they truly contribute to lasting economic advancement (Wharton, 1999).

We end with this final statement:

I ask that you always keep in mind that successful answers must reflect a framework of values that places the sanctity and aspirations of the individual human being at the heart of what the U.S. role in the world should be. We have to, once again, begin seeing the world as a planet of human beings – not as abstractions tied solely to national security concerns such as nonproliferation or nationalism and ethnic hatreds or gaining trade advantage. We must recognize that it all begins with people (Wharton, 1993).

13 Concluding Comments

This study has attempted to provide some insight into the contributions of black economists. The economists selected for this study include some very controversial individuals, some of whom have not traditionally been viewed as economists. Each individual included herein, however, was trained as an economist.

The study notes the contributions of early African philosophers such as St. Augustine of Algeria and Eratosthenes of Alexandria. For too long, the contributions of black economists have been overlooked.

The economists examined in this study include Nobel Laureate Sir W. Arthur Lewis, Kwame Nkrumah, W. E. B. Du Bois, Thomas Sowell, Walter Williams, Glenn Loury, William Darity, Jr., Andrew Brimmer, Clifton Wharton, Jr., and Phyllis Wallace. All of these individuals made contributions to economics.

Arguably, the greatest contributor and one of the least controversial is Sir W. Arthur Lewis, a leading growth theorist who won the Nobel Prize in 1979. The next is the great African statesman, Kwame Nkrumah, who served as president of Ghana and propounded theories criticizing imperialism. W. E. B. Du Bois, trained as an economist in the German Historical vein, advanced the theory of the Talented Tenth for the upliftment of African-Americans. Thomas Sowell's and Walter Williams' stand against affirmative action has made them two of the more controversial black economists today. Glenn Loury's middle-of-the-road views have tended to ostracize him. Andrew Brimmer is the more mainstream and most influential black economist today. William Darity, Jr. continues to conduct empirical studies. Clifton Wharton, Jr., despite his few contributions to the theory, is nonetheless a potent force. Phyllis Wallace, the lone female in this study, is also worthy of emulation.

To understand these economists and their contributions, it is important to realize that they wrote about the times in which they live(d). So, then, what are the lessons learned from this seminal study?

- Economics is a broad field of study that involves sociological and political observations. Economics does not deal only with money; it goes much further. Economics is a dynamic and intricate discipline that deals with both the positive and normative. It is erroneous to assume that economics has to do only with empirical investigation and is devoid of value. Economics is a social science and, as such, deals with human behavior. Thus, economists tend to provide prescriptions.

• The study of economics can lead to careers in a great number of fields. The study of economics does not limit one to analysis of data or careers in industry. As we have seen, although all of the individuals in this study were trained as economists, they utilized that training to venture into politics (Nkrumah), government service (Wallace and Wharton), journalism (Williams), and academia. Economics is about analytical thinking and involves the ability to think critically and the application of logic to any process. The scholars described in this study have proven that economics is worth studying.

• A great many African scholars have not been given their just due. As indicated earlier, many African scholars have not received credit for their scholarship. We do not attempt to claim that the Egyptian, Libyan and other scholars were necessarily black, only that they were African in origin. Whether or not they were of Greek origin is not the issue; it is the African connection that is important. It is also important to realize that no culture develops in a vacuum. Consequently, there is some interdependence between geographically contiguous cultures. As ancient Greece influenced Egypt, so Egypt influenced Greece. In spite of that, there is no excuse for claiming African scholars such as Eratosthenes and Euclid as Greek. St. Augustine and other scholastics made long-lasting and significant contributions to the ancient scholarship. Mercantilism was exploitative and led to colonialism and the African slave trade. The first 'school' of economics – mercantilism – was exploitative. In fact, it could be renamed exploitationism. The mercantilist quest for gold led to the establishment of colonies in Africa and other areas, and eventually to the African slave trade. The 'free' slave labor ensured that raw materials flowed into Europe at a cheap price to facilitate the production of finished goods to be exported for more gold bullion. Any discussion of mercantilism must include a discussion of the slave trade, the most economically exploitative event in the history of mankind.

• Black economists have mattered. Economic thought tends to classify economists according to the schools to which they belong or according to their theoretical area. Unfortunately, of all the economists in this study,

only Lewis is included in the standard text. This is because he was
strictly an economic theorist by profession and won the Nobel Prize.
Many of the others, such as Nkrumah, Du Bois and Wharton, mixed their
economics with politics and sociology; consequently, they were multi-
disciplinary and, in some instances, controversial. Thus, it has been
difficult to view them as economists. In spite of that, these individuals
were economists who propounded economic theories. In the case of
Williams, Sowell, Brimmer, Loury, Darity and Wallace, their economic
pronouncements have focused specifically on race issues. Because this
is not mainstream economics, it is not likely to appear in standard texts.
Also, issues of race and the underclass are not theoretical enough.
Thanks to these individuals, however, such discussions are becoming
more and more a part of mainstream economics. Nkrumah brought the
concept of imperialism to the forefront; Du Bois made race and human
capital important issues in the African-American community; Sowell and
Williams espoused alternative ways of regarding race issues; Loury
chose a different approach; Darity and Brimmer have provided empirical
analyses with different conclusions from that of Sowell and Williams;
Wallace brought the studies of the black female worker into economics;
and Wharton concentrated on the international picture. All of these
individuals have made noteworthy contributions to the field and deserve
credit for it.

• It is imprudent to criticize or vilify those individuals whose views we
  consider controversial without first trying to understand them. It appears
  that people are quick to criticize without first seeking to understand. It is
  easy to misconstrue someone's ideas in that sense. We avoided labeling
  individuals in this study as conservatives or liberals. We attempted to
  relate their views to schools of economics (neo-classical, monetary), not
  political stereotypes. By so doing, we are able to present the individual's
  views objectively and in a non-biased manner. Conceptually, this
  facilitates the theoretical understanding and one is able to glean the
  merits and demerits of the arguments more objectively and rationally.
  This study is replete with such examples – Du Bois' debates with
  Washington and Garvey; the views of Sowell and Williams on
  affirmative action; and Loury's affirmative action stance. Were we to
  take time to truly and objectively evaluate these views, most would
  realize that although we may not agree with them in their totality, they do
  in many instances make economic (and common) sense. Unfortunately,
  we may regard them from a biased and 'politically correct' viewpoint

and dismiss them outright without due consideration. It is hoped that this study has shed more light on these controversial views to allow for more dialogue and understanding. Case in point, Sowell and Williams are not against the black community; *au contraire*, they are for the betterment of the black community. Just because they may not agree with other black intellectuals does not make their views and contributions any less valid for black upliftment. Just because someone does not agree with us does not necessarily make that individual either wrong or a traitor. This is perhaps the most important lesson to be learned from this study.

• Most circumstances, situations or conditions have more than one cause. The fallacy of single causation tends to be insular and provincial. We subscribe to the theory of multiple causation. For example, to say that blacks have made little progress only because of discrimination or lack of education is too restrictive. It is more appropriate and sensible to attribute the condition of blacks to a multitude of factors, including discrimination and lack of human capital. This is the scholarly way of viewing any situation.

• Human capital is the key to black economic development. The common theme pervading the views of all of the economists in this study is that in order for blacks to make progress, they must develop human capital and skills. Du Bois' concept of the Talented Tenth is a human capital concept, and all the others speak to it in one way or another. In order for blacks to continue to make progress, the focus must be on education in all its variant forms. Humanity is important. Economic development cannot be successfully pursued while neglecting the masses. The 'haves' need to always remain cognizant of the 'have-nots.' This is the way to economic progress. As Wharton appropriately states (1993):

> I ask that you always keep in mind that successful answers must reflect a framework of values that places the sanctity and aspirations of the individual human being at the heart of what the U.S. role in the world should be. We have to, once again, begin seeing the world as a planet of human beings – not as abstractions tied solely to national security concerns such as nonproliferation or nationalism and ethnic hatreds or gaining trade advantage. We must recognize that it all begins with people.

As we study economics, we must keep an inquisitive and open mind while realizing that through its evolution, it has had numerous contributors, many of whom were in the minority.

Bibliography

Chapter 1

Amacher, R.C. and Ulbrich, H.H. (1992), *A Cheerful Look at the Dismal Science – Opportunities in Economics*, Southwestern Publication Co., Cincinnati, Ohio.

Case, K.E. and Fair, R.C. (1999), *Principles of Economics*, 5th ed., Prentice Hall, New Jersey.

Hewins, W.A.S. (1910), *The Encyclopedia Britannica*, The University Press, Cambridge, England.

Marshall, A. (1920), *Principles of Economics*, 8th ed., Macmillan of Canada, Ontario.

Parkin, M. (1998), *Economics*, 4th ed., Addison-Wesley, Reading, Massachusetts.

Rees, A. (1968), in D. Sills (ed), *International Encyclopedia of the Social Sciences*, vol. 4, The Macmillan Company and The Free Press, New York.

Samuelson, P.A. and Nordhaus, W.D. (1998), *Economics*, 16th ed., Irwin McGraw Hill, Boston.

Sedgwick, H. (1987), in J. Eatwell, M. Milgate and P. Newman (eds), *The New Palgrave: A Dictionary of Economics*, vol. 2, The Macmillan Press Limited, London.

Viner, J. (1937), *Studies in the Theory of International Trade*, Harper, New York.

Chapter 2

Akomolafe, F. (1998), *Review of George B. M. James's Stolen Legacy*, Web Publishing, Hartford, Connecticut.

Alic, M. (1986), *Hypatia's Heritage: A History of Women in Science from Antiquity to the Late Nineteenth Century*, The Women's Press Limited, London.

Allen, W.R. (1970), 'Modern Defenders of Mercantilist Theory', *History of Political Economy*, vol. 2, pp. 381-397.

Berlinerblau, J. (1996), 'Black Athena Revisited', *The Nation*, vol. 263(13), pp. 42-46.

Bernal, M. (1987), *Black Athena: The Afroasiatic Roots of Classical Civilization*, 46. Vintage, London.

Bernal, M. and Moore, D.C. (1997), *Black Athena Writes Back: Martin Bernal Responds to His Critics*, Duke University Press, Durham, North Carolina.

'Blacks are Key to World Progress, Historian Asserts' (1995, May 9) (electronic version), *Philadelphia Tribune*. Available:
http://emeagwali.com/special/black-scientists/black-inventors.html.

Blaug, M. (ed) (1991), *The Early Mercantilists*, Edward Elgar, Brookfield, Vermont.

Brue, S.L. (1994), *The Evolution of Economic Thought*, 5th ed., The Dryden Press, Fort Worth, Texas.

Catholic Encyclopedia (electronic version), available: www.newadvent.org/cathen.

Columbia Encyclopedia, 5th ed. (1995), (electronic version), available: www.slider.com/enc.

Compton's Encyclopedia Online. The Learning Company, Fremont, California.

Diop, C.A. (1967), *The African Origin of Civilization: Myth or Reality*, Lawrence Hill and Co., Westport, Presence Africaine, Paris.

Diop, C.A. (1985), 'Africa's Contribution to World Civilization: The Exact Sciences', in I. Van Sertima (ed), *Nile Valley Civilizations: Proceedings of the Nile Valley Conference, Atlanta, Sept. 26-30, 1984*, Journal of African Civilizations, New Brunswick, New Jersey.

Ekelund, R.B., Jr. (1997), *A History of Economic Theory and Method*, 4th ed., The McGraw Hill Companies, Inc., New York.

Garvey, M. and Garvey, A.J. (1963), *Philosophy and Opinions of Marcus Garvey*, vol. 1 (reprint of 1923 edition), Julian Richardson Associates, San Francisco.

Hall, C.A. (1998), 'Augustine Who?', *Christianity Today*, vol. 42(6), pp. 66-67.

Hart, G. (ed) (1990), *Ancient Egypt*, Dorling Kindersley, London.

Lefkowitz, M. (1992), 'Not Out of Africa: The Origins of Greece and Illusions of Afrocentrists', *The New Republic*, vol. 206(6), pp. 29-36.

List, F. (1966), S. Lloyd (tr), *National System of Political Economy* (translation of 1841 edition), F. Cass, London.

Malaty, T.Y. (1995), *The School of Alexandria, Book 2*, On-line, available: http://www.saintmark.com/topics/patrology/schoolofalex2/.

McCaskell, T.A. (1994), *A History of Racism*, Toronto Board of Education, Toronto.

Morrison, P. and Morrison, P. (1989), *The Ring of Truth*, Vintage Books, New York.

Pantheon of the World Brotherhood of Light: A Tribute to the Memory of the Greatest Heros in World History, On-line, available: http://www.sangha.net/messengers/.

Roncaglia, A. (1985), *Petty: The Origin of Political Economy*, M.E. Sharpe, Armonk, New York.

Schumpeter, J.A. (1981), *History of Economic Analysis*, Oxford University Press, New York.

Segal, R. (1967), *The Race War*, Viking Press, New York.

'St. Anthony the Great', On-line, available: http://www.studentgroups.ucla.copic/sayings/storyofstanthony.html.

'St. Gregory the Wonderworker', On-line, available: http://cygnus.uwa.edu.au/~jgrapsas/pages/gregory.htm.

'St. Moses the Black', On-line, available: http://www.snc.edu/norbertines/mosesblack.html.

'The Trans-Atlantic Slave Trade: From Africa to Europe', On-line, available: http://library.thinkquest.org/13406/contents.html?tqskip1=1&tqtime=0612.

'Theodorus of Cyrene', On-line, available: http://turnbull.dcs.st-and.ac.uk/history/Mathematicians/Theodorus.html.

True, P., Jr. (ed), 'An Overview of Black History', On-line, available: http://www.nbufront.org/html/MastersMuseums/JHClarke/WorldHistoryOvervie w/WorldHistoryOverview.html.

Van Sertima, I. (1976), *They Came Before Columbus*, Random House, New York.

Ziniewicz, G.L. (1997), 'Cyrenaic Guidelines', On-line, available: http://www.fred.net/tzaka/cyrenaic.html.

Chapter 3

Bigelow, B.C. (ed) (1993), *Contemporary Black Biography: Profiles from the International Black Community*, vol. 3, Gale Research, Inc., Detroit, Michigan.

Brue, S.L. (1994), *The Evolution of Economic Thought*, 5th ed., The Dryden Press, Fort Worth, Texas.

Case, K.E. and Fair, R.C. (1999), *Principles of Economics*, 5th ed., Prentice Hall, New Jersey.

Du Bois, W.E.B. (1899), *The Philadelphia Negro: A Special Study*, University of Pennsylvania.

Du Bois, W.E.B. (1903), *The Souls of Black Folk: Essays and Sketches*, A.C. McClurg.

Du Bois, W.E.B. (1909), *John Brown*, G.W. Jacobs.

Du Bois, W.E.B. (1920), *Darkwater: Voices from within the Veil*, Harcourt, New York.

Du Bois, W.E.B. (1924), *The Gift of Black Folk – The Negroes in the Making of America*, Stratford Co.

Du Bois, W.E.B. (1928), *Dark Princess: A Romance*, Harcourt, New York.

Du Bois, W.E.B. (1935), *Black Reconstruction: An Essay Toward a History of the Part Which Black Folk Played in the Attempt to Reconstruct Democracy in America, 1860-1880*, The Free Press, New York.

Du Bois, W.E.B. (1939), *Black Folk, Then and Now: An Essay in the History and Sociology of the Negro Race*, Holt, New York.

Du Bois, W.E.B. (1940), *Dusk of Dawn: An Essay toward an Autobiography of a Race Concept*, Harcourt, New York.

Du Bois, W.E.B. (1945), *Color and Democracy: Colonies and Peace*, Harcourt, New York.

Du Bois, W.E.B. (1947), *The World and Africa: An Inquiry into the Part Which Africa Has Played in World History*, Viking, New York.

Du Bois, W.E.B. (1957), *The Ordeal of Mansart* (Part I of the *Flame Trilogy*), Mainstream Publishers.

Du Bois, W.E.B. (1959), *Mansart Builds a School* (Part II of the *Flame Trilogy*), Mainstream Publishers.

Du Bois, W.E.B. (1961), *Worlds of Color* (Part III of the *Flame Trilogy*), Mainstream Publishers.

Du Bois, W.E.B. (1968), *The Autobiography of W. E. B. Du Bois: A Soliloquy on Viewing My Life from the Last Decade to Its First Century*, International Publishers, New York.

Du Bois, W.E.B. (1975), *The Negro*, Thompson Organization Limited, New York.

Du Bois, W.E.B. (1985), and H. Aptheker (ed), *Against Racism*, The University of Massachusetts Press, Amherst.

Du Bois, W.E.B. (1989), *The Souls of Black Folk*, Bantam Books, New York.

Ekelund, R.B., Jr. and Hebert, R.F. (1997), *A History of Economic Theory and Method*, The McGraw Hill Companies, Inc., New York.

Foner, P.S. (ed) (1970), *W. E. B. Du Bois Speaks: Speeches and Addresses 1890-1919*, Pathfinder Press, New York.

Green, M. (1998), *The Debate Over African American Education: W. E. B. Du Bois and Booker T. Washington*, Cobblestone Publishing, Peterborough.

Halsey, W.D. and Johnston, B. (eds) (1986), *Colliers Encyclopedia*, vol. 13 and 20, MacMillan Publishing Co., New York.

Hewins, W.A.S. (1910), *The Encyclopedia Britannica*, The University Press, Cambridge, England.

Lomax, M.L. (1998), *Tapping Two Educational Roots: A Document in a Blending of the Educational Philosophies of Booker T. Washington and W. E. B. Du Bois*, Crisis Publishing Company, Incorporated, New York.

Marable, M. (1986), *W. E. B. Du Bois: Black Radical Democrat*, Twayne Publishers, Boston.

McKissack, P. and McKissack, F. (1990), *W. E. B. Du Bois*, Franklin Watts, New York.

McKissack, P., McKissack, F., and Bryant, M. (1992), *Booker T. Washington: Leader and Educator*, Enslow Publisher, Inc., Berkeley Heights.

Moseley-Braun, C. (1995), *Between W. E. B. Du Bois and Booker T. Washington: A Personal Development Discipline – How Moseley-Braun was Raised in a Family that did not Acknowledge or Legitimize Racism*, Johnson Publishing Company, Chicago.

Rees, A. (1968), in D. Sills (ed), *International Encyclopedia of the Social Sciences*, vol. 4, The Macmillan Company and The Free Press, New York.

Schumpeter, J.A. (1981), *History of Economic Analysis*, Oxford University Press, New York.

Sedgwick, H. (1987), in J. Eatwell, M. Milgate and P. Newman (eds), *The New Palgrave: A Dictionary of Economics*, vol. 2, The Macmillan Press Limited, London.

Washington, B.T. (1901), *Up From Slavery: An Autobiography*, Bantam Books, New York.

Washington, B.T. and Du Bois, W.E.B. (1901), *The Great Divide: Booker T. Washington and W. E. B. Du Bois Debate How to Prosper the Black Race*, American Enterprise Institute for Public Policy Research, Washington, DC.

Chapter 4

Blaug, M. (1985), *Great Economists Since Keynes: An Introduction to the Lives of 100 Modern Economists*, Cambridge University Printers, Cambridge.

Breit, W. and Spencer, R.W. (1997), *Lives of the Laureates: Thirteen Nobel Economists*, MIT Press, Cambridge, Massachusetts.

Brue, S.L. (1994), *The Evolution of Economic Thought*, 5th ed., The Dryden Press, Fort Worth, Texas.

Caribbean Studies Association Conference (1989), 'Sir Arthur Lewis: The Simplicity of Genius', Caribbean Studies Association, Barbados.

Chenery, H. and Srinivasan, T.N. (eds) (1995), *Handbook of Development Economics*, Elsevier Science Publishing Co., New York.

Ellis, G. (1987), *Sir Arthur Lewis*, Imprint Caribbean, San Juan, Trinidad.

Fishlow, A. (1995), 'Future Sustainable Latin American Growth: A Need for Savings', *The Review of Black Political Economy*, vol. 24(1), pp. 7-21.

Frimpong-Ansah, J.H. (1987, September), *Professor Sir W. Arthur Lewis: A Patriarch of Development Economics*, Paper presented at the annual conference of the Development Studies Association, University of Manchester.

Houseman, G.L. and Maung, A (1992), 'Understanding World Economic Development: The Work of W. Arthur Lewis', *Challenge*, vol. 35, pp. 60-61.

Kanth, R.K. (1994), *Paradigms in Economic Development: Classic Perspectives, Critiques, and Reflections*, M. E. Sharpe, Armonk, New York.

Lalljie, R. (1996), *Sir Arthur Lewis, Nobel Laureate: A Biographical Profile*, R. Ferdinand-Lalljie, Castries, St. Lucia.

Lewis, W.A. (1949), *The Principles of Economic Planning*, D. Dobson, London.

Lewis, W.A. (1965), *Politics in West Africa*, Allen and Unwin, London.

Lewis, W.A. (1980), 'Autobiography of Sir Arthur Lewis', On-line, available: http://www.nobel.se/economics/laureates/1979/lewis-autobio.html.

Lewis, W.A. (1983), *Selected Economic Writings of W. Arthur Lewis*, New York University Press, New York.

Lewis, W.A. (1994), *Sir William Arthur Lewis: Collected Papers, 1941-1988*, University of the West Indies, Institute of Social and Economic Research (Eastern Caribbean), Cave Hill, Barbados.

Lewis, W.A. (1994), 'The Face of Man: Perspectives on the Economic, Social, Cultural and Political Development of the Caribbean', The Dr. Eric Williams Memorial Lectures, Central Bank of Trinidad and Tobago, Port of Spain.

Lewis, W.A. and Barker, T.E., et al (1982), *Perspectives on Economic Development: Essays in the Honour of W. Arthur Lewis*, University Press America, Washington, DC.

Promdas, R. and St. Cyr, E. (1991), *Sir Arthur Lewis: An Economic and Political Portrait*, University of the West Indies, Regional Programme of Monetary Studies, Institute of Social and Economic Research, Mona, Jamaica.

Rostow, W.W. (1990), *Theorists of Economic Growth from David Hume to Present*, Oxford University Press, London.

Wilkinson, A. (1994), *Sir William Arthur Lewis: A Bibliographical Portrait*, Institute of Social and Economic Research, Barbados.

Chapter 5

Addo, E.O. and Nugent, P. (1999), 'Shorter Notices – Kwame Nkrumah', *Africa*, vol. 69(4), p. 660.

Afari-Gyan, K. (1985), *Nkrumah's Ideology*, University of Ghana, Legon, Ghana.

Alex-Hamah, J. (1983), *Farewell Africa: Life and Death of Nkrumah*, Times Press, Lagos.

Amissah, G.M. (1983), *Living Echoes of Kwame Nkrumah*, Mfantsiman Press, Cape Coast, Ghana.

Arhin, K. (1990), *A View of Kwame Nkrumah, 1909-1972: An Interpretation*, Sedco Publishing Ltd., Accra, Ghana.

Assensoh, A.B. (1989), *Kwame Nkrumah of Africa: His Formative Years and the Beginning of His Political Career, 1935-1948*, Stockwell, Ilfracombe.

Babatope, E. (1978), *Nkrumaism Revisited*, Abiprint & Pak, Lagos.

Bigelow, B.C. (ed) (1993), *Contemporary Black Biography: Profiles from the International Black Community*, vol. 3, Gale Research, Inc., Detroit, Michigan.

Birmingham, D. (1990), *Kwame Nkrumah*, Cardinal, London.

Birmingham, D. (1998), *Kwame Nkrumah: The Father of African Nationalism*, Ohio University Press, Athens.

Birmingham, D. (1998), 'Nkrumah as 'Small Boy' – Review of Kwame Nkrumah: The Years Abroad, 1935-1947', *Journal of African History*, vol. 39(1), pp. 160-161.

Birmingham, D. and Sherwood, K. (1999), 'Book Reviews – Kwame Nkrumah: The Father of African Nationalism', *The International Journal of African Historical Studies*, vol. 32(1), p. 151.

Blay, J. B. (1973), *Legend of Kwame Nkrumah*, Abicom Ltd., Accra, Ghana.

Boateng, C.A. (1995), *Nkrumah's Consciencism: An Ideology for Decolonization and Development*, Kendall/Hunt Publishing Co., Dubuque, Iowa.

Botchway, F. (1970), *Politics as Drama: Philosophy and Opinions of Dr. Kwame Nkrumah*, Black Academy Press, Buffalo, New York.

Budu-Acquah, K. (1992), *Kwame Nkrumah: The Visionary*, Service and Method Agency, Accra, Ghana.

Crisis (1999), 'Third World Visionaries of the 20th Century', vol. 106(4), pp. 42-44.

Davidson, B. (1989), *Black Star: A View of the Life and Times of Kwame Nkrumah*, Westview Press, Boulder, Colorado.

Dzirasa, S. (1961), *Political Thought of Dr. Kwame Nkrumah*, Guinea Press, Accra, Ghana.

Essack, K. (1990), *In Defence of Kwame Nkrumah*, Thakers, Dar es Salaam.

Gyan, A. (1976), *The Political Ideas of Kwame Nkrumah*, African Heritage Studies Publishers, New York.

Haynes, J. (1999), 'Reviews - Selected Speeches of Kwame Nkrumah as compiled by Samuel Obeng', *The Journal of Modern African Studies*, vol. 37(3), pp. 507-581.

James, C.L.R. (1964), *Nkrumah Then and Now*, University Place Bookshop, New York.

James, C.L.R. (1982), *Nkrumah and the Ghana Revolution*, Allison and Busby, London.

Jarmon, C. (1981), *The Nkrumah Regime: An Evaluation of the Role of Charismatic Authority*, Brunswick Publishing Co., Lawrenceville, Virginia.

Johnson, C.X. (1994), *Ghana Under Nkrumah*, C.X. Johnson, Chicago.

Krafona, K. (1993), *A.B.C. of Nkrumaism*, Afroworld Publishing Co., London.

Leman, D. (1994), 'Kwame Nkrumah: The Conakry Years', *Canadian Journal of African Studies*, vol. 28(2), p. 343.

Marais, G. (1972), *Kwame Nkrumah As I Knew Him*, Janay Publishing Co., Chichester.

Moukoko Mbonjo, P. (1998), *The Political Thought of Kwame Nkrumah: A Comprehensive Presentation*, University of Lagos Press, Lagos.

Nkrumah and State Enterprises (1985), Symposium on the Life and Work of Kwame Nkrumah, University of Ghana, Institute of African Studies, Legon, Ghana.

Nkrumah, K. (1957), *Ghana: The Autobiography of Kwame Nkrumah: Black Star*, Thomas Nelson, New York.

Nkrumah, K. (1965), *Autobiography*, T. Nelson, New York.

Nkrumah, K. (1968), *Dark Days in Ghana*, 2nd ed., International Publishers, New York.

Nkrumah, K. (1970), *12 Key Speeches of Kwame Nkrumah*, African Publication Society, London.

Nkrumah, K. (1973), *Axioms of Kwame Nkrumah; Freedom Fighters' Edition*, International Publishers, New York.

Nkrumah, K. (1973), *Revolutionary Path*, Panaf Books Ltd., London.

Nkrumah, K. (1976), *I Speak of Freedom: A Statement of African Ideology*, Greenwood Press, Westport, Connecticut.

Nkrumah, K. (1990), *Kwame Nkrumah: The Conakry Years, His Life and Letters*, PANAF, London.

Nkrumah, K. (1997), *Selected Speeches*, Afram Publications Ltd., Accra, Ghana.

Okadigbo, C. (1985), *Consciencism in African Political Philosophy: Nkrumah's Critique*, Fourth Dimension Publishers, Enugu, Nigeria.

Omari, T.P. (1970), *Kwame Nkrumah: The Anatomy of an African Dictatorship*, Moxon Paperbacks, Accra, Ghana.

Osundina, O. (1978), *Kwame Nkrumah of Ghana: A Bibliography on His Works and Life*, National Library of Nigeria, Lagos.

Phillips, J.F.V. (1960), *Kwame Nkrumah and the Future of Africa*, Praeger, New York.

Sherwood, M. and Brempong, N.A. (1998), 'Book Reviews – Kwame Nkrumah: The Years Abroad, 1935-1947', *The International Journal of African Historical Studies*, vol. 31(2), p. 429.

Smertin, Y. (1990), *Kwame Nkrumah*, Progress Publishers, Moscow.

State Publishing Company (1966), *What Was Wrong With Nkrumah*, Accra, Ghana.

Timothy, B. (1955), *Kwame Nkrumah, His Rise to Power*, G. Allen & Unwin, London.

Toure, A.S. (1972), *Promotion Kwame Nkrumah*, Pratrice Lumumba, S.I., Imprimerie Nationale.

Ture, K. (1998), 'Kwame Ture on Kwame Nkrumah', *The Crisis*, vol. 105(3), p. 44.

Van Sertima, I. (1988), *Great Black Leaders: Ancient and Modern, Journal of African Civilizations*, vol. 9, New Brunswick, New Jersey.

Chapter 6

Anderson, A. and Bark, D (eds) (1988), *Thinking About America: The United States in the 1990s*, Hoover Institution Press, Stanford, California.

Appiah, K.A. (1995), 'Review – Race and Culture: A World View by Thomas Sowell', *The New York Review of Books*, vol. 42(1), p. 29.

Bigelow, B.C. (ed) (1992), *Contemporary Black Biography: Profiles from the International Black Community*, vol. 2, Gale Research, Inc., Detroit, Michigan.

Boston, T. D. (1996), 'Review of *Race and Culture* by Thomas Sowell', *Journal of Economic Literature*, vol. 34(1), pp. 163-165.

Boxx, T.W. (1994) and G.M. Quinlivan (ed), *The Cultural Context of Economics and Politics*, University Press of America, Lanham, Maryland.

Brimelow, P. (1998), 'Human Capital', *Forbes*, vol. 162(1), pp. 52-58.

Brue, S.L. (1994), *The Evolution of Economic Thought*, 5th ed., The Dryden Press, Fort Worth, Texas.

Conti, J.G. (1993), *Challenging the Civil Rights Establishment: Profiles of a New Black Vanguard*, Praeger, Westport, Connecticut.

Coren, M. (1995), 'At Last – A Hardheaded, Hopeful View on Race: A Review of *Race and Culture* by Thomas Sowell', vol. 22(15), pp. 47-48.

Fischel, J. (1998), 'The Dilemma of Diversity', *Virginia Quarterly Review*, vol. 47(3), pp. 564-568.

Gatti, P.L. (1981), *The Limits of Government Regulation*, Academic Press, New York.

Groff, P. (1994), 'Inside American Education: The Decline, The Deception, The Dogmas by Thomas Sowell', *The Freeman*, vol. 44(6).

Henderson, D.R. and Sowell, T. (1999), 'Booktalk – Race and Economics', *The American Enterprise*, vol. 10(5), pp. 80-84.

Mead, L. (1992), *The New Politics of Poverty: The Non-working Poor in America*, Basic Books, New York.

Moch, L.P. (1999), 'Review of *Migrations and Cultures: A World View* by Thomas Sowell', *Journal of Social History*, vol. 33(1), pp. 209-211.

Mokyr, J. (1998), 'The Secrets of Success', *Reason*, vol. 30(7), pp. 70-71.

Nash, R.J. (1995), 'A Neo-essentialist Diatribe Against American Education', *Journal of Teacher Education*, vol. 46(2), pp. 150-155.

Pagden, A. (1998), 'Culture Wars', *New Republic*, vol. 219(20), pp. 36-42.

Puddington, A. (1990), 'Preferential Policies, by Thomas Sowell', *The American Spectator*, vol. 23(11), pp. 44-45.

Robinson, F. (1995), 'Review of the *Vision of the Anointed: Self-Congratulation as a Basis of Social Policy* by Thomas Sowell', *National Minority Politics*, vol. 7(12), p. 36.

Robson, J.S.P. (1996), 'Ever Wonder Why Nobody's Listening, a Review of *A Conflict of Vision: Ideological Origins of Political Struggles* by Thomas Sowell', *Alberta Report/Newsmagazine*, vol. 23(22), p. 44.

Robson, J.S.P. (1998), 'A Rare Good Word for Military Conquest', *Albert Report/Newsmagazine*, vol. 25(38), pp. 36-37.

Skerry, P. (1996), 'Second Thoughts About Immigration', *Public Interest*, no. 125, pp. 132-135.

Sowell, T. (1971), *Economics: Analysis and Issues*, Scott Foresman, Glenview, Illinois.

Sowell, T. (1972), *Black Education: Myths and Tragedies*, McKay, New York.

Sowell, T. (1975), *Affirmative Action Reconsidered: Was It Necessary in Academia?*, American Enterprise Institute for Public Policy Research, Washington, DC.

Sowell, T. (1975), *Race and Economics*, Longmans, New York.

Sowell, T. (1976), *Dissenting From Liberal Orthodoxy: A Black Scholar Speaks For The 'Angry Moderates'*, American Enterprise Institute for Public Policy Research, Washington, DC.

Sowell, T. (1977), *Patterns of Black Excellence*, Ethics and Public Policy Center, Washington, DC.

Sowell, T. (1978), *American Ethnic Groups*, Urban Institute, Washington, DC.

Sowell, T. (1978), *Essays and Data on American Ethnic Groups*, Urban Institute, Washington, DC.

Sowell, T. (1980), *Knowledge and Decisions*, Basic Books, New York.

Sowell, T. (1981), *Ethnic America: A History*, Basic Books, New York.

Sowell, T. (1981), *Markets and Minorities*, Basil Blackwell for the International Center for Economic Policy Studies, Oxford.

Sowell, T. (1981), *Markets and Minorities*, Basic Books, New York.

Sowell, T. (1983), *The Economics of Politics and Race*, Quill and W. Morrow, New York.

Sowell, T. (1986), *Education: Assumptions Versus History: Collected Papers*, Hoover Institution Press, Stanford, California.

Sowell, T. (1987), *Conflict of Vision: Ideological Origins of Political Struggle*, Quill and W. Morrow, New York.

Sowell, T. (1990), *Preferential Policies: An International Perspective*, 1st ed., Quill and W. Morrow, New York.

Sowell, T. (1991), *Cultural Diversity: A World View*, American Enterprise Institute for Public Policy Research, Washington, DC.

Sowell, T. (1991), *Racial Preference and Racial Justice: The New Affirmative Action Controversy*, Ethics and Public Policy Center, Washington, DC.

Sowell, T. (1991, August 21), *The Washington Times*.

Sowell, T. (1991, September 6), 'Burying Black Differences Under Labels and Myths', *Orange County Register*.

Sowell, T. (1993), *Is Reality Optional? And Other Essays*, Hoover Institution Press, Stanford, California.

Sowell, T. (1994), *Classical Economics Reconsidered*, Princeton University Press, Princeton, New Jersey.

Sowell, T. (1994), *From Different Shores: Perspectives on Race and Ethnicity in America*, 2nd ed., Oxford University Press, New York.

Sowell, T. (1995), 'Somebody Has to Pay for Everything – One Way or Another', *National Minority Politics*, vol. 7(10), p. 16.

Sowell, T. (1995), 'Why the Poor Stay Poor', *Alberta Report Newsmagazine*, vol. 22(29), p. 27.

Sowell, T. (1996), *Knowledge and Decisions*, Basic Books, New York.

Sowell, T. (1996), *Migrations and Cultures: A World View*, Basic Books, New York.

Sowell, T. (1997), *Affirmative Action: Social Justice or Reverse Discrimination?*, Prometheus Books, Amherst, New York.

Sowell, T. (1998), *Conquests and Cultures: An International History*, Hi Marketing, London.

Sowell, T. (1998), *Race, Culture and Equality*, Hoover Institution on War, Revolution and Peace, Stanford, California.

Sowell, T. (1999), *Barbarians Inside the Gates – And Other Controversial Essays*, Hoover Institution Press, Stanford, California.

Sowell, T. (1999), *The Quest for Cosmic Justice*, Free Press, New York.

Sowell, T. (2000), 'Transcript – Words Worth Repeating – Thomas Sowell Attacks Educational 'Fairness' That is Unjust to Those it Aids', *The American Enterprise*, vol. 11(2), p. 46.

Williams, W.E. (1998), 'Why Aren't Eskimos Great Farmers? A Review of Thomas Sowell's Conquests and Cultures', *Human Events*, vol. 54(37), p. 16.

Chapter 7

Bigelow, B.C. (ed) (1993), *Contemporary Black Biography: Profiles from the International Black Community*, vol. 4, Gale Research, Inc., Detroit, Michigan.

Conti, J.G. (1993), *Challenging the Civil Rights Establishment: Profiles of a New Black Vanguard*, Praeger, Westport, Connecticut.

George Mason University, Department of Economics, On-line, available: http://www.gmu.edu/departments/economics.

Leighton, G.S. (1991), 'South Africa's War Against Capitalism', *International Journal on World Peace*, vol. 8(3), pp. 89-91.

Walter Williams, On-line, avail.: http://www.gmu.edu/departments/economics/wew.

'Williams, Jr., W. E.' (1993), *Williams and Mary Law Review*, vol. 34(2), p. 333.

Williams, W.E. (1990), 'Free Enterprise', *Success*, vol. 37(6), p. 16.

Williams, W.E. (1993), 'Adventures of the Mind: The State of the Mind that Promotes Wealth', *The Saturday Evening Post*, vol. 265(1), p. 33.

Williams, W.E. (1993), 'Africa Must Reject Leftism', *Human Events*, vol. LIII(3), p. 13.

Williams, W.E. (1993), 'Anti-Poverty Programs Opposed by Government', *Human Events*, vol. LII(42), p. 12.

Williams, W.E. (1993), 'Big-Government Assault on the Family', *Human Events*, vol. LIII(13), p. 14.

Williams, W.E. (1993), 'Blacks Can't Count on Government', *Human Events*, vol. LIII(41), p. 8.

Williams, W.E. (1993), 'Costly and Needless Regulations', *Human Events*, vol. LIII(15), p. 13.

Williams, W.E. (1993), 'Government Can't Solve Blacks' Problems', *Human Events*, vol. LIII(49), p. 14.

Williams, W.E. (1993), 'Government 'Cure'', *Human Events*, vol. LIII(44), p. 15.

Williams, W.E. (1994), 'Civil Rights Leaders Ignore Reality', *Human Events*, vol. 50(19), p. 15.

Williams, W.E. (1994), 'Liberal Blame-Game Not Solving Illiteracy', *Human Events*, vol. 50(49), p. 15.

Williams, W.E. (1995), 'A Tragic Vision of Black Problems', *American Quarterly*, vol. 47(3), pp. 409-415.

Williams, W.E. (1995), 'Bureaucratic 'Assistance' Keeps Poor Unemployed', *Human Events*, vol. 51(1), p. 16.

Williams, W.E. (1995), 'Capitalism Fosters Equal Opportunity', *Human Events*, vol. 51(17), p. 15.

Williams, W.E. (1995), 'Rights Versus Wishes', *National Minority Politics*, vol. 7(7), p. 17.

Williams, W.E. (1995), 'Sex, Families, Race, Poverty, Welfare', *The American Enterprise*, vol. 6(1), p. 33.

Williams, W.E. (1995), 'The Argument for Free Markets: Morality vs. Efficiency', *The Cato Journal*, vol. 15(2), p. 179.

Williams, W.E. (1995), 'Unappreciated Miracles', *National Minority Politics*, vol. 7(10), p. 17.

Williams, W.E. (1996), 'Racial and Sexual Discrimination', *The St. Croix Review*, vol. 29(2), p. 21.

Williams, W.E. (1996), 'The Welfare Debate', *Society*, vol. 33(5), p. 13.

Williams, W.E. (1998), 'The Pursuit of Happiness – Discrimination and Liberty', *The Freeman*, vol. 48(4), p. 255.

Williams, W.E. (1998), 'Welfare in the Workplace', *Regulation*, p. 73.

Chapter 8

Appiah, K.A. (1995), 'What Kind of Bootstraps, a Review of *One by One From the Inside Out: Essays and Reviews on Race and Responsibility in America* by Glenn C. Loury', *Wilson Quarterly*, vol. 19(3), p. 77.

Boston University, 'Biography of Glenn C. Loury', On-line, available: http://www.bu.edu/irsd/loury/lourybio.htm.

Conti, J.G. (1993), *Challenging the Civil Rights Establishment: Profiles of a New Black Vanguard*, Praeger, Westport, Connecticut.

Cromartie, M. (1996), 'Conquering the Enemy Within', *Christianity Today*, vol. 40(1), p. 17.

Donlon, J.P. (1995), 'The Road Back', *Chief Executive*, no. 107, p. 6.

Freedman, S.G. (1998), 'Is The Drug War Racist? An Interview with Glenn Loury', *Rolling Stone*, no. 786, p. 35.

'Glenn Loury's Moment' (1996), *Economist*, vol. 340(7973), p. 32.

Herbert, W. (1995), 'The End of Discussion?', *U. S. News & World Report*, vol. 119(13), p. 18.

Herbert, W. (1995), 'The Fate of Racism, a Review of *One by One From the Inside Out: Essays and Reviews on Race and Responsibility in America* by Glenn C. Loury', *U. S. News & World Report*, vol. 119(11), p. 93.

Krugman, P. (1998), 'Glenn Loury's Round Trip: The Trials and Temptations of a Black Intellectual', On-line, avail.: http://www.bu.edu/irsd/articles/dismal.htm.

Loury, G.C. (1976), *Essays in the Theory of the Distribution of Income*, Unpublished doctoral dissertation, Massachusetts Institute of Technology.

Loury, G.C. (1977), 'A Dynamic Theory of Racial Income Differences', in P. Wallace (ed), *Women, Minorities and Employment Discrimination*, Lexington Books, Lanham, MD.

Loury, G.C. (1981), 'Intergenerational Transfers and the Distribution of Earnings', *Econometrica*, vol. 49(4).

Loury, G.C. (1985), *Glenn Loury – The Crisis in Black America*, National Public Radio, Washington, DC.

Loury, G.C. (1987), *A Conservative Agenda for Black Americans*, Heritage Foundation, Washington, DC.

Loury, G.C. (1987), *Glenn C. Loury, Professor of Political Economics,* Harvard University, John F. Kennedy School of Government, Video-Stg., Sunnyvale, California.

Loury, G.C. (1988), *Welfare Return: Consensus or Conflict?*, University Press of America and National Forum Foundation, Lanham, Maryland.

Loury, G.C. (1989), *The Question of Discrimination: Racial Inequality in the U.S. Labor Market*, Wesleyan University Press, Middletown, Connecticut.

Loury, G.C. (1990), *Achieving the 'Dream': A Challenge to Liberals and to Conservatives in the Spirit of Martin Luther King, Jr.,* Heritage Foundation, Washington, DC.

Loury, G.C. (1992), 'Incentive Effects of Affirmative Action', *Annals of the American Academy of Political and Social Science*, no. 523, pp. 19-29.

Loury, G.C. (1993), *Ghetto Poverty and the Power of Faith*, Center of the American Experiment, Minneapolis, Minnesota.

Loury, G.C. (1993), *Self-Censorship in Public Discourse: A Theory of 'Political Correctness' and Related Phenomena*, Boston University, Department of Economics, Boston.

Loury, G.C. (1994), 'The Alliance Is Over', *Moment*, vol. 19(3), p. 32.

Loury, G.C. (1994), 'The Poverty of Reason', *The A. M. E. Church Review*, no. 356, p. 12.

Loury, G.C. (1995), 'A Professor's Transformation: One Man's Dramatic Journey from Spiritual Death to New Life', *The American Enterprise*, vol. 6(6), pp. 29-30.

Loury, G.C. (1995), 'Individualism Before Multiculturalism', *The Public Interest*, no. 121, pp. 92-106.

Loury, G.C. (1995), *One by One from the Inside Out: Essays and Reviews on Race and Responsibility in America*, Free Press, New York.

Loury, G.C. (1995), 'One Man's March', *The New Republic*, vol. 213(19), pp. 18-21.

Loury, G.C. (1995), 'Sex, Families, Race, Poverty, Welfare', *The American Enterprise*, vol. 6(1), p. 33.

Loury, G.C. (1996), 'Can Professors Help the Poor?', *Planning for Higher Education*, vol. 24(2), p. 70.

Loury, G.C. (1996), 'Joy and Doubt on the Mall. The New Republic', *The Utne Reader*, no. 73, pp. 70-73.

Loury, G.C. (1996), *Reducing Poverty in America: Views and Approaches*, Sage Publications, Thousand Oaks, California.

Loury, G.C. (1996), *The Affirmative Action Debate*, Perseus Books, Reading, MA.

Loury, G.C. (1996), *The Divided Society and the Democratic Idea*, Boston University, Boston.

Loury, G.C. (1997), 'Head to Head', *The Crisis*, vol. 104(3), p. 22.

Loury, G.C. (1997), 'How to Mend Affirmative Action', *The Public Interest*, no. 127, pp. 33-43.

Loury, G.C. (1997), 'How to Mend Affirmative Action' (electronic version), *The Public Interest*, available: http://www.bu.edu/irsd/articles/howtomnd.htm.

Loury, G.C. (1997), 'The Hard Questions: Comparative Disadvantage', *The New Republic*, vol. 217(15), p. 29.

Loury, G.C. (1997), 'The Hard Questions: Double Talk', *The New Republic*, vol. 217(8), p. 23.

Loury, G.C. (1997), 'The Hard Questions: Exclusionary Rule', *The New Republic*, vol. 217(21), pp. 13-14.

Loury, G.C. (1997), 'The Hard Questions: Pride and Prejudice', *The New Republic*, vol. 216(20), p. 25.

Loury, G.C. (1998), 'A Symposium: Is Affirmative Action on the Way Out? Should It Be?', *Commentary*, vol. 105(3), pp. 38-39.

Loury, G.C. (1998), 'An American Tragedy: The Legacy of Slavery Still Lingers in Our Cities' Ghettos', *The Brookings Review*, vol. 16(2), pp. 38-42.

Loury, G.C. (1998), 'Discrimination in the Post-Civil Rights Era: Beyond Market Interactions', *The Journal of Economic Perspectives*, vol. 12(2), pp. 117-126.

Loury, G.C. (1998), *Economics, Ethics and Public Policy*, Rowman & Littlefield, Lanham, Maryland.

Loury, G.C. (1998), *Glenn C. Loury: Selected Clips, January 1997-March 1998*, Boston University, Institute on Race and Social Division, Boston, Massachusetts.

Loury, G.C. (1998), 'The Hard Questions: Color Blinded', *The New Republic,* vol. 219(7/8), p. 12.

Loury, G.C. (1998), 'The Hard Questions: Uneconomical', *The New Republic*, vol. 218(26), pp. 14-15.

Loury, G.C. (1998), 'The Hard Questions: Uneconomical' (electronic version), *The New Republic*, available: http://www.bu.edu/irsd/articles/uneconomical.htm.

Loury, G.C. (1998), 'The Hard Questions: Unequalized', *The New Republic*, vol. 218(14), pp. 10-11.

Loury, G.C. (1998), 'The Hard Questions: Welfare Pair', *The New Republic*, vol. 218(1/2), pp. 9-10.

Loury, G.C. (1999), *The African-American Predicament*, Brookings Institution Press, Washington, DC.

Nuechterlein, J. (1996), 'Neocon Agonites' Review of *One by One from the Inside Out: Essays and Reviews on Race and Responsibility in America* by Glenn C. Loury', *Public Interest*, no. 122, p. 125.

Podhoretz, N. (1999), 'The Loyalty Trap', *National Review*, vol. 51(1), p. 32.

Robinson, F. (1995), 'Review of *One by One from the Inside Out: Essays and Reviews on Race and Responsibility in America* by Glenn C. Loury', *National Minority Politics*, vol. 7(7), p. 36.

Rodriquez, R. (1997), 'The Other', *The American Enterprise,* vol. 8(3), p. 34.

'The Agony of Glenn Loury' (1997) (editorial), *National Review*, vol. 49(24), p. 17.

Chapter 9

African-Americans (1993), Auburn House, Westport, Connecticut.

Binswanger, H.P. and Williams, W.A., Jr. (1999), 'Money and Magic: A Critique of the Modern Economy in the Light of Goethe's Faust', *History of Political Economy*, vol. 31(1), pp. 207-208.

Campbell, D.A. and Warner, J.M. (1997), 'Formally Modelling a Gender-Segregated Economy: A Response to William Darity, Jr.', *World Development*, vol. 25(12), pp. 2155-2158.

Cherry, R. (1992), 'The Question of Discrimination: Racial Inequality in the U. S. Labor Market,' *The Review of Radical Political Economics*, vol. 24(2), p. 150.

Darity, W.A., Jr. (1965), *Poverty*, University of North Carolina, Westminster Fellowship, Chapel Hill, North Carolina.

Darity, W.A., Jr. (1980), *Black Economic Progress*, University of Wisconsin, Institute for Research on Poverty, Madison, Wisconsin.

Darity, W.A., Jr. (1982), *Race, Poverty, and the Urban Underclass*, Lexington Books, Lexington, Massachusetts.

Darity, W.A., Jr. (1984), *A Kalecki-Keynes Model of World Trade, Finance, and Economic Growth*, Board of Governors of the Federal Reserve System, Washington, DC.

Darity, W.A., Jr. (1988), *The Loan Pushers: The Role of Commercial Banks in the International Debt Crisis*, Ballinger Publishing Co., Cambridge, Massachusetts.

Darity, W.A., Jr. (1990), 'British Industry and the West Indies Plantations', *Social Science History*, vol. 14(1), p. 117.

Darity, W.A., Jr. (1990), *The Wealth of Races*, Greenwork Press, New York.

Darity, W.A., Jr. (1991), *Black-White Earnings Gaps Have Widened*, University of Maryland at College Park, Afro-American Studies Program, College Park, Maryland.

Darity, W.A., Jr. (1992), *The Atlantic Slave Trade*, Duke University Press, Durham, North Carolina.

Darity, W.A., Jr. (1993), *Interethnic Disparity Across Census Divisions: 1980-1990*, University of North Carolina at Chapel Hill, Old Dominion University, Chapel Hill, North Carolina.

Darity, W.A., Jr. (1993), *Labor Economics: Problems in Analyzing Labor Markets*, Kluwer Academic, Boston.

Darity, W.A., Jr. (1994), 'Who Owns Maynard Keynes?', *History of Political Economy*, vol. 26(1), pp. 155-164.

Darity, W.A., Jr. (1995), 'Comment – The Diffusion of the Keynesian Revolution: The Young and the Graduate Schools', *History of Political Economy*, vol. 27, pp. 243-246.

Darity, W.A., Jr. (1995), *The Decline in Marriage Among African Americans*, Russell Sage Foundation, New York.

Darity, W.A., Jr. (1995), 'The Formal Structure of a Gender-Segregated Low-income Economy', *World Development*, vol. 23(11), pp. 1963-1968.

Darity, W.A., Jr. (1995), 'The Undesirables, America's Underclass in the Managerial Age', *Daedalus' Proceedings of the American Academy of Arts and Sciences*, vol. 124(1), p. 145.

Darity, W.A., Jr. (ed) (1995), *Economics and Discrimination*, vol. 1 and 2, Aldershot, Brookfield, Vermont.

Darity, W.A., Jr. (1997), *Civil Rights and Race Relations in the Post Reagan-Bush Era*, Praeger, Westport, Connecticut.

Darity, W.A., Jr. (1997), 'Formally Modelling a Gender-Segregated Economy', *World Development*, vol. 25(12), p. 2159.

Darity, W.A., Jr. (1998), 'Evidence on Discrimination in Employment: Codes of Color, Codes of Gender', *The Journal of Economic Perspectives*, vol. 12(2), p. 63.

Darity, W.A., Jr. (1998), 'Intergroup Disparity: Economic Theory and Social Science Evidence', *Southern Economic Journal*, vol. 64(4), p. 805.

Darity, W.A., Jr. (1998), 'Racial Earnings Disparities and Family Structure', *Southern Economic Journal*, vol. 65(1), p. 20.

Darity, W.A., Jr. (1999), 'Roundtable on Employment Policy – Who Loses from Unemployment', *Journal of Economic Issues*, vol. 33(2), p. 491.

Darity, W.A., Jr. and Brewer, D.J. (1996), 'Labor Economics: Problems in Analyzing Labor Markets', *Industrial & Labor Relations Review*, vol. 49(2), p. 366.

Darity, W.A., Jr. and Goldsmith, A.H. (1993), 'Unemployment, Social Psychology, and Unemployment Hysteresis', *Journal of Post Keynesian Economics*, vol. 16(1), p. 55.

Darity, W.A., Jr. and Goldsmith, A.H. (1996), 'Social Psychology, Unemployment and Macroeconomics', *The Journal of Economic Perspectives*, vol. 10(1), p. 121.

Darity, W.A., Jr. and Myers, S.L. (1998), *Persistent Disparity: Race and Economic Inequality in the United States Since 1945*, Edward Elgar, Northampton, Massachusetts.

Darity, W.A., Jr., Dietrich, J., and Guilkey, D.K. (1997), 'Racial and Ethnic Inequality in the United States: A Secular Perspective', *The American Economic Review*, vol. 87(2), p. 301.

Darity, W.A., Jr., Guilkey, D.K., and Winfrey, W. (1995), 'Ethnicity, Race, and Earnings,' *Economics Letters*, vol. 47, pp. 401-408.

Darity, W.A., Jr., Guilkey, D.K., and Winfrey, W. (1996), 'Explaining Differences in Economic Performance Among Racial and Ethnic Groups in the USA: The Data Examined', *American Journal of Economics and Sociology*, vol. 55(4), pp. 411-425.

Darity, W.A., Jr., Myers, S.L., Jr., and Carson, E.D. (1994), *The Black Underclass: Critical Essays on Race and Unwantedness (Critical Studies in Black Life and Culture, vol. 27)*, Garland Publishing, New York.

Darity, W.A., Jr., Myers, S.L., Jr., and Galbraith, J.K. (1999), 'Book Reviews – Persistent Disparity: Race and Economic Inequality in the United States Since 1945', *Southern Economic Journal*, vol. 66(2), p. 493.

Dimand, R.W., Darity, W.A., Jr., and Young, W. (1997), 'Reply to 'Hawtrey and the Multiplier'', *History of Political Economy*, vol. 29(3), p. 557.

Goldsmith, A.H., Veum, J.K., and Darity, W.A., Jr. (1997), 'The Impact of Psychological and Human Capital on Wages', *Economic Inquiry*, vol. 35(4), p. 815.

Leiman, M.M., and Darity, W.A., Jr. (1995), 'Political Economy of Racism', *Journal of Economic Literature*, vol. 33(3), p. 1374.

Parcel, T.L., Shulman, S., and Darity, W.A., Jr. (eds) (1992), 'The Questions of Discrimination: Racial Inequality in the U.S. Labor Market', *Contemporary Sociology*, vol. 21(6), p. 791.

Shulman, S. and Darity, W.A., Jr. (eds) (1989), *The Question of Discrimination: Racial Inequality in the U.S. Labor Market*, 1st ed., Wesleyan University Press, Middletown, Connecticut.

Thomas, R.J. (1998) and Darity, W.A., Jr. (ed), 'Economics and Discrimination', *Ethnic and Racial Studies*, vol. 21(4), p. 780.

Thorton, R.J. (1994) and Darity, W.A., Jr. (ed), 'Labor Economics: Problems in Analyzing Labor Markets', *The Journal of Risk and Insurance*, vol. 61(4), p. 735.

'William A. Darity, Jr.', On-line, avail: www.cpc.unc.edu/pubs/review98/darity.html.

Chapter 10

'Andrew F. Brimmer', On-line, Horatio Alger Association of Distinguished Americans, available: www.horatioalger.com/member/bri74.htm.

Bigelow, B.C. (ed) (1992), *Contemporary Black Biography: Profiles from the International Black Community*, vol. 2, Gale Research, Inc., Detroit, Michigan.

'Black America Today', *Encyclopedia Americana/CBS News Audio Resource Library*, New York.

Brimmer, A.F. (1951), *Some Economic Aspects of Fair Employment*, M.A. thesis/dissertation, University of Washington.

Brimmer, A.F. (1955), *The Setting of Entrepreneurship in India*, Massachusetts Institute of Technology, Center for International Studies, Cambridge, Massachusetts.

Brimmer, A.F. (1962), *Life Insurance Companies in the Capital Market*, Michigan State University, Bureau of Business and Economic Research, Graduate School of Business, East Lansing, Michigan.

Brimmer, A.F. (1967), *Bank Credit Cards and Check-Credit Plans: Development and Implications*, Board of Governors of the Federal Reserve System, San Francisco.

Brimmer, A.F. (1967), *International Capital Markets and the Financing of U.S. Foreign Trade and Investment*, Remarks at the 30th Chicago World Trade Conference, Chicago.

Brimmer, A.F. (1969), *The Banking System and Urban Economic Development*, Board of Governors of the Federal Reserve System, Washington, DC.

Brimmer, A.F. (1970), *The Black Banks*, The American Finance Association, Detroit, Michigan.

Brimmer, A.F. (1971), *Bank Credit Cards: the Record of Innovation and Growth*, Board of Governors of the Federal Reserve System, Washington, DC.

Brimmer, A.F. (1971), *The Neglected Black Majority*, Randolph Educational Fund, New York.

Brimmer, A.F. (1972), *Multi-national Banks and the Management of Monetary Policy in the United States*, American Economic Association, Toronto.

Brimmer, A.F. (1972), *Recent Developments in Black Banking: 1970-1971*, Board of Governors of the Federal Reserve System, Washington, DC.

Brimmer, A.F. (1973), *Andrew Brimmer on Unemployment and Teen Wage*, Joint Center for Political Studies, Washington, DC.

Brimmer, A.F. (1973), *Employment and Income in the Black Community: Trends and Outcomes*, University of California, Institute of Government and Public Affairs, Los Angeles.

Brimmer, A.F. (1974), *Prospects for Commercial Banks in International Money and Capital Markets: An American Perspective*, Board of Governors of the Federal Reserve System, Washington, DC.

Brimmer, A.F. (1974), *Public Utility Pricing, Debt Financing, and Consumer Welfare*, Remarks, Board of Governors of the Federal Reserve System, Washington, DC.

Brimmer, A.F. (1976), *Business and the American Economy*, New York University Press, New York.

Brimmer, A.F. (1976), *Economic Development: International and African Perspectives*, Associated Publishers, Washington, DC.

Brimmer, A.F. (1976), *The Economic Position of Black Americans*, National Commission for Manpower Policy, Washington, DC.

Brimmer, A.F. (1977), *U. S. Long-Term Economic Outlook Implications for the Black Consumer Market*, Brimmer and Co., Washington, DC.

Brimmer, A.F. (1979), *Public Utility Pricing, Debt Financing, and Consumer Welfare*, Remarks, Board of Governors of the Federal Reserve System, Washington, DC.

Brimmer, A.F. (1982), *Blacks in the American Economy*, Brimmer and Co., Washington, DC.

Brimmer, A.F. (1982), *Monetary Policy and the International Diffusion of Interest Rates*, Florida International University, International Banking Center and Department of Economics, Miami, Florida.

Brimmer, A.F. (1985), *The World Banking System: Outlook in a Context of Crisis*, New York University Press, New York.

Brimmer, A.F. (1985), *Trends, Prospects, and Strategies for Black Economic Progress*, Joint Center for Political Studies, Washington, DC.

Brimmer, A.F. (1990), '45 Years in Business and Employment', *Ebony*, vol. XLVI(1), pp. 123-124.

Brimmer, A.F. (1992), 'The Dilemma of Black Banking: Lending Risks vs. Community Service', Lecture, *The Review of Black Political Economy*, vol. 20(3), pp. 5-31.

Brimmer, A.F. (1993), *Economic Cost of Discrimination Against Black Americans*, Brimmer and Co., Washington, DC.

Brimmer, A.F. (1995), 'Economic Cost of Discrimination Against Black Americans', in M.V.L. Badgett and M.C. Simms (eds), *Economic Perspectives on Affirmative Action*, Joint Center for Political and Economic Studies, Washington, DC.

Brimmer, A.F. (1998), 'Long-term Trends and Prospects for Black-owned Businesses', *The Review of Black Political Economy*, vol. 26(1), pp. 19-36.

Vise, D.A. (1995, June 8), 'Chairman Draws Curtain on D. C. Control Board', *Washington Post*, p. A01.

Vise, D.A. (1997, August 9), 'For Brimmer, D.C. Had But One Way Out', *Washington Post*, p. A01.

Chapter 11

Anderson, B. (1994), 'The Economic Status of African-American Women – Special Session in Honor of Phyllis A. Wallace', *American Economic Review*, vol. 84(2), pp. 91-92.

Delongoria, M. and Wallace, P.A. (1994), *Phyllis Ann Wallace: A Black Woman Economist and Public Policy*, M.A. thesis/dissertation, Morgan State University.

Mabunda, L.M. (ed) (1995), *Contemporary Black Biography: Profiles from the International Black Community*, vol. 9, Gale Research, Inc., Detroit, Michigan.

Malveaux, J. (1994), 'Tilting Against the Wind: Reflections on the Life and Work of Phyllis Ann Wallace', *American Economic Review*, vol. 84(2), pp. 93-97.

Wallace, P.A. (1967), *Employment Patterns in the Drug Industry, 1966*, Equal Employment Opportunity Commission, Washington, DC.

Wallace, P.A. (1967), *Testing of Minority Group Applicants for Employment*, Equal Employment Opportunity Commission, Office of Research and Reports, Washington, DC.

Wallace, P.A. (1974), *Pathways to Work: Unemployment Among Black Teenage Females*, D. C. Health, Lexington, Massachusetts.

Wallace, P.A. (1980), *Black Women in the Labor Force*, MIT Press, Cambridge, Massachusetts.

Wallace, P.A. (1981), *Social Issues in Collective Bargaining 1950-1980: A Critical Assessment*, Massachusetts Institute of Technology, Alfred P. Sloan School of Management, Cambridge, Massachusetts.

Wallace, P.A. (1982), *Black Women in the Labor Force*, 1st ed., MIT Press, Cambridge, Massachusetts.

Wallace, P.A. (1982), *Women in the Workplace*, Auburn House Publishing Co., Boston.

Wallace, P.A. (1984), *Title VII and the Economic Status of Blacks*, Massachusetts Institute of Technology, Alfred P. Sloan School of Management, Cambridge, Massachusetts.

Wallace, P.A. (1985), *The Private Sector and Equal Employment Opportunity in the 1980s*, Massachusetts Institute of Technology, Industrial Relations Section, Alfred P. Sloan School of Management, Cambridge, Massachusetts.

Wallace, P.A. (1985), *Upward Mobility of Young Managers: Women on the Fast Track?*, Massachusetts Institute of Technology, Alfred P. Sloan School of Management, Cambridge, Massachusetts.

Wallace, P.A. (1989), *MBAs on the Fast Track: The Career Mobility of Young Managers*, Ballinger Publishing Co., New York.

Wallace, P.A. (1990), *Affirmative Action from a Labor Market Perspective*, Massachusetts Institute of Technology, Alfred P. Sloan School of Management, Cambridge, Massachusetts.

Chapter 12

Bigelow, B.C. (ed) (1994), *Contemporary Black Biography: Profiles from the International Black Community*, vol. 7, Gale Research, Inc., Detroit, Michigan.

Branch, S. and Edmond, A., Jr. (1993), 'Clifton Wharton, Jr.', *Black Enterprise*, vol. 23(7), p. 134.

Clarke, C.V. and Lowery, M. (1994), 'What's Next for Clifton Wharton?', *Black Enterprise*, vol. 24(11), p. 30.

Metcalf, G.R. (1971), *Up From Within: Today's New Black Leaders*, 1st ed., McGraw-Hill, New York.

Nelson A. Rockefeller Institute of Government (1993), *Clifton R. Wharton, Jr.*, State University of New York, Albany, New York.

'Not So Silent Partner' (1990), Interview with Clifton Wharton, *Chief Executive*, no. 63, pp. 40-43.

'Reflections of a Trailblazer' (1998), Interview with Dr. Clifton R. Wharton, Jr., *Black Issues in Higher Education*, vol. 15(6), pp. 14-17.

Thompson, K.W. (1983), *Institutions for Projecting American Values Abroad*, University Press of America, Lanham, Maryland.

Wharton, C., Jr. (1963), *The Economic Meaning of 'Subsistence'*, Agricultural Development Council, New York.

Wharton, C., Jr. (1969), *Subsistence Agriculture and Economic Development*, Aldine Publishing, Chicago.

Wharton, C., Jr. (1970), 'Clifton Wharton Delivers a Speech at Detroit Economic Club on Higher Education, Universities', Recording, Michigan State University.

Wharton, C., Jr. (1980), *Statement of Dr. Clifton R. Wharton, Jr., Chancellor, State University of New York, before the Joint Senate Committee on Finance and the Assembly Ways and Means Committee, February 25, 1980*, The State University of New York, Albany, New York.

Wharton, C., Jr. (1983), *Testimony of Dr. Clifton R. Wharton, Jr., Chancellor, State University of New York before a Joint Hearing of the Assembly Ways and Means Committee, Senate Finance Committee, March 1, 1983*, State University of New York, Albany, New York.

Wharton, C., Jr. (1989), *The New America*, CED, Washington, DC.

Wharton, C., Jr. (1990), 'Reflections on Poverty', *American Journal of Agricultural Economics*, vol. 72(5), pp. 1131-1138.

Wharton, C., Jr. (1993), 'A New Generation and America's Post-Cold War Challenges', Commencement Address Delivered at American University, *U. S. Department Dispatch*, vol. 4(20), p. 349.

Wharton, C., Jr. (1993), 'Clifton Wharton, Jr. Takes his Education, Business and Economics Background to World Arena', *Black Issues in Higher Education*, vol. 9(23), p. 6.

Wharton, C., Jr. (1993), *Testimony of the Honorable Clifton R. Wharton, Jr., before the Senate Foreign Relations Subcommittee on International Economic Policy Trade, Oceans and Environment, July 14, 1993*, Washington, DC.

Wharton, C., Jr. (1993), 'USAID and Foreign Aid Reform', *U. S. Department of State Dispatch*, vol. 4(30) p. 526.

Wharton, C., Jr. (1994), 'Preventive Diplomacy: Redefining National Security', *The Educational Record*, vol. 75(2), p. 57.

Wharton, C., Jr. (1995), 'The Myth of Superpower', *Vital Speeches of the Day*, vol. 61(7), p. 204.

Wharton, C., Jr. (1999), 'Human Capital and Socio-Cultural Values', *Vital Speeches of the Day*, vol. 65(9), pp. 276-280.

Wharton, C., Jr., Lorsch, J.W., and Hanson, L. (1991), 'Advice and Dissent: Rating the Corporate Governance Compact', *Harvard Business Review*, vol. 69(6), pp. 136-145.

Index